DID MOHAWKS
WEAR MOHAWKS?

DID MOHAWKS WEAR MOHAWKS?

And Other Wonders, Plunders, and Blunders

BRUCE TINDALL AND MARK WATSON

QUILL

WILLIAM MORROW

New York

Grateful acknowledgment is made for excerpts from the following sources:

From *Nimmer on Copyright* by Melville B. Nimmer and David Nimmer, copyright © 1989 by Matthew Bender & Co., Inc.

From *Introduction to Parasitology in Tropical Africa* by F.M.A. Ukoli. Copyright © 1984 by John Wiley & Sons. Reprinted by permission of the publisher.

From *America: A Narrative History* by George Brown Tindall. Copyright © 1984 by W. W. Norton & Co., Inc. Reprinted by permission of the publisher.

From *A Fundamental Survey of the Moon* by R. B. Baldwin. Copyright © 1965 by McGraw-Hill, Inc. Reprinted by permission of the publisher.

From *The Eiffel Tower* by Joseph Harriss. Copyright © 1975 by Joseph Harriss. Reprinted by permission of Grafton Books.

From *Inner Asian Frontiers of China* by Owen Lattimore. Copyright © 1940 by the American Geographical Society. Reprinted by permission of the American Geographical Society.

From *Foundations of Parasitology* by Gerald D. Schmidt and Larry S. Roberts. Copyright © 1989 by Times Mirror/Mosby College Publishers. Reprinted by permission of C. V. Mosby Co.

From "My Geophagy Problem—and Yours" by Roy Blount, Jr. Copyright © 1987 by Roy Blount, Jr. Reprinted by permission of *The Atlantic Monthly* and the author.

Excerpt from the *Oxford English Dictionary*, 2nd ed. Copyright © 1989 by Oxford University Press. Reprinted by permission of the publisher.

From *The C.N.D. Story* by John Minnion and Philip Bolsover. Copyright © 1983 by John Minnion and Philip Bolsover. Reprinted by permission of Allison and Busby Publishers.

From "Early Defectors in March to Aldermaston." Copyright © 1958 by Manchester Guardian and Evening News, Ltd. Reprinted by permission of *The Guardian* newspaper.

From *The Ecology of Stray Dogs* by Alan Beck. Copyright © 1973 by Alan M. Beck. Reprinted by permission of York Press.

From *The Naval Aviation Guide*, 2nd ed., by Rear Adm. Malcolm W. Cagle. Copyright © 1969 by the United States Naval Institute. Reprinted by permission of the U.S. Naval Institute Press.

From "Sleep Well" in the "TRB" column, *New Republic*. Copyright © 1969 by Harrison-Blaine of New Jersey, Inc. Reprinted by permission of *The New Republic*.

From *Flying the Oceans: A Pilot's Story of Pam Am, 1935–1955*, 3rd ed., by Horace Brock. Copyright © 1978 by Horace Brock. Reprinted by permission of Jason Aronson Inc., Publishers.

From *Charles Richard Drew* by Charles E. Wyners. Copyright © 1988 by Board of Trustees of the University of Illinois. Reprinted by permission of the University of Illinois Press.

From "The Limited Nutritional Value of Cannibalism" by Stanley Garn and Walter Block in *American Anthropologist*. Copyright © 1970 by Stanley M. Garn and Walter D. Block. Reprinted by permission of Stanley M. Garn.

From *The Disney Version* by Richard Schickel. Copyright © 1986 by Richard Schickel. Reprinted by permission of Pavilion Books and the author.

From *Political Frontiers and Boundaries* by J.R.V. Prescott. Copyright © 1987 by J.R.V. Prescott. Reprinted by permission of Unwin Hyman, Ltd.

From *The Camel and the Wheel* by Richard W. Bulliet. Copyright © 1975 by The President and Fellows of Harvard College. Reprinted by permission of Harvard University Press.

From "Litigating Copyright Cases" by Russell J. Frackman in *Litigating Copyright, Trademark, and Unfair Competition Cases 1987*. Copyright © 1987 by Practicing Law Institute. Reprinted by permission of Practicing Law Institute.

Library of Congress Cataloging-in-Publication Data

Tindall, Bruce.
   Did Mohawks wear Mohawks?: and other wonders, plunders, and blunders by Bruce Tindall and Mark Watson.
      p.   cm.
   ISBN 0-688-09859-2
   1. Curiosities and wonders.   I. Watson, Mark.   II. Title.
AG243.T44   1991
031.02—dc20
                                                                                                        90–49009
                                                                                                        CIP

Printed in the United States of America

First Quill Edition

1 2 3 4 5 6 7 8 9 10

BOOK DESIGN BY PAUL CHEVANNES

Contents

Introduction

WONDERS, plunders, and blunders. Infotainment. Q. & A. "Lite" information. Whatever you call them, books like this one have fascinated readers from the days of the ancient Greeks up to the present.

It all started with Herodotus, the Greek writer born in 484 B.C., who traveled the world and wrote about the marvels he saw or heard tell of. For centuries, historians were skeptical of some of Herodotus's unlikely tales, but recent archaeological research has proven many of his stories true.

In ancient Rome, and throughout Europe during the Middle Ages, people read the *Natural History* of Pliny the Elder with its descriptions of fabulous beasts and strange peoples. Although many of his statements turned out to be incorrect, they were at least entertaining. Pliny never stopped doing research to discover more facts: He was killed by noxious volcanic fumes in A.D. 79 as he was investigating an eruption of Mt. Vesuvius.

Book buyers in the 1850s eagerly snapped up volumes like *Things Not Generally Known,* which answered such questions as "How many times do an insect's wings beat each second?" and "Is it legal for a minister to officiate at his own wedding?" In our own day, even movie star Michael Caine has gotten into the act with his book

Most People Don't Know That. Every book of this kind that's published only seems to whet the readers' appetite for more.

So—here's more! There are *wonders:* things you may always have wondered about (like the title question), and things you may *never* have wondered about (like "Why did they build the Great Wall of China?"—it wasn't for the reason you probably think).

There are *plunders:* pirate raids, plagiarism of popular songs, and the notorious salami scam.

There are *blunders:* the Susan B. Anthony dollar coin, medical research disasters, civil defense boondoggles, and worst of all, the new Coca-Cola.

And there are all sorts of other fascinating things. There's high tech (how do weightless astronauts go to the bathroom?) and low tech (ancient first aid). There are the heavens (Will the moon fall on us someday?) and the earth (how they make borders). There's the modern day (the latest scientific data from the moon) and olden times (who invented the wheel?). There's medicine (what causes cold headaches?), law (how not to make a citizen's arrest), and theology (who's the patron saint of the public relations profession?). There's language (the difference between gray and grey, or twelve and a dozen), music (how to make a castrato), and sports (Olympic tiddlywinks?). There are even horseshoes *and* hand grenades.

You'll learn what to do when giant worms crawl out of your nostrils, who John Doe was, and how to identify a hoon—a single one or a whole gaggle. You'll be able to dazzle your friends by singing the *real* words to the national anthem at the next football game. You'll make the acquaintance of Tvyordy Znak, the Duke of Earl, Mountbars the Exterminator, and a real live dobby looms pegger. And those of you who have a freezer full of human corpses or flamingo tongues are in luck: We have recipes for you!

Read on, enjoy, and be sure to see our invitation to you at the end of the book.

Cannibalism: A Poor Source of Fiber

CANNIBALS are people who eat other people. But what *parts* of other people? And what are some of their favorite recipes?

Before answering those questions, we need to know if there really is such a thing as cannibalism in the first place. Of course, stranded travelers and shipwrecked sailors have eaten human flesh in emergencies, and it is well established that some societies occasionally perform symbolic acts of cannibalism. But some anthropologists say they can find no credible evidence that any society has ever regularly eaten people for nourishment.

Although dietary cannibalism may not actually exist, almost every society in the world tells *stories* about cannibalism, according to anthropologist William Arens. For example, when Europeans began exploring the interior of Africa, many of them brought back tales of cannibal tribes. Conversely, some Africans told stories about strange white-skinned men who had come to steal and eat babies. For some reason, Arens says, people around the world label societies they don't understand as cannibalistic.

If there are any full-time cannibals, they probably have a hard time keeping their pantries stocked. Researchers Stanley Garn and Walter Block published a scholarly paper in 1979 showing that it would not be wise to rely on human flesh as a regular, significant source of protein. They estimated that a 110-pound man "might yield 30 kilograms [66 pounds] of edible muscle mass if skillfully butchered." This much meat would contain the minimum daily requirement of protein for about sixty people. "One man, in other words, serves 60, skimpily." If this little clan of sixty ate nothing but humans, it would need a new victim every day. Even if the group used human flesh merely as a protein supplement, Garn and Block concluded, it would have to eat about its own number of people every year.

Still, the anthropological literature is full of descriptions of cannibalism (although these often begin with a phrase like: "I did not observe this myself, but a tribal elder told me . . ."). Some researchers have devised elaborate schemes for classifying different kinds of cannibalism, such as alimentary, warrior, ritual-crime, pathological/curative, and pathological/erotic types. Another approach classifies the practice not according to its purpose but its victim: endo-cannibalism (eating members of one's own group), exo-cannibalism (eating strangers), and auto-cannibalism (eating oneself).

Eating the flesh and heart of an enemy, especially if he died after prolonged torture, in order to gain his bravery and strength has been practiced by warriors in several parts of the world. In one such case, Iroquois Indians tore the flesh from a man's arms and legs while he still lived and roasted it. They eventually killed the victim by tearing out his heart, then roasted and ate that, too. But not all Iroquois approved of cannibalism, and in 1756 the Iroquois League outlawed it.

Funeral rites in some societies involve cannibalism. Among the Bimin-Kuskusmin people of New Guinea, relatives of the deceased may ceremonially eat a bit of his bone marrow, belly fat, and, for the widow, a sliver of penis.

Accounts like these don't bother the anthropologists who

say there's no such thing as dietary cannibalism. Such cases, they say, are infrequent rituals and don't prove that anybody eats other people primarily *for food*.

In any event, researchers and explorers have collected a few recipes for human flesh (which tastes like pork, and which some Polynesian languages call "long pig"). The Bimin-Kuskusmin eat enemies killed in battle (especially the heart and genitals), sometimes cooked, sometimes raw. The Aztecs ate war captives, boiled, carved, and served over corn with a little salt but without chilies. Even cannibals, though, have taste. The Bimin-Kuskusmin dislike brains and the contents of the intestines and are especially repelled by gallbladder. They say it "fouls the taste" of the human meat. Australian aborigines and the Maori of New Zealand are said to have preferred the taste of their own people to the saltier flesh of Europeans.

What Makes Tiddlers Wink?

O NE day around 30 B.C., some Chinese military officers gave their ruler, Cheng-di, some advice. Stop playing football, they said. (Ancient Chinese football, called *zuju*, was similar to soccer and used a leather ball filled with hair.) It's too exhausting, they warned him, and dangerous. Besides, they admonished, it's undignified for the emperor to play such games.

His Majesty took their advice but became despondent at the loss of his favorite recreation. His wife had an idea to cheer him up, though: If you can't play football, play tiddlywinks instead.

Emperor Cheng-di set the precedent, but the tradition of tiddling royalty continues to the present day. At a British tiddlywinks tournament in 1958, gamesmen from Oxford and Cambridge universities competed against other tiddlers, including a team called the Goons, sponsored by Prince Philip, husband of the queen. The prince himself had planned to take part, but as he told the audience, "Unfortunately, while practicing secretly, I pulled an important muscle in the second, or tiddly, joint of my winking finger."

A spokesman for the British students told reporters, with a straight face, that he and his fellows were trying to have tiddlywinks represented officially in the 1960 Olympic Games. They didn't succeed, but they did manage to organize some international competition on their own. In 1962, Oxford defeated Harvard. Later that year, in the first all-American affair, Harvard beat Holy Cross while the band played "Fair Harvard" and a crowd of forty-three cheered the tiddlers on.

The words *tiddly* and *tiddlywinks* have had varied careers and existed long before they were applied to the game they now denote. *Tiddly* has been used to mean both "drunk" and "tidy." *Tiddlywink* was Cockney rhyming slang for "drink" and, by extension, came to mean an unlicensed bar, or the British equivalent of a speakeasy. The first known use of the word in reference to the game was in 1857.

There's controversy at the highest intellectual levels over the exact spelling of the word. At the British tournament, the Oxonians said they were "tiddlers" who played "tiddlewinks," while the Cantabrigian players called themselves "winkers" and the game, "tiddlywinks." *Tiddleywinks* and *tiddle-a-wink* have also been used.

You may think of tiddlywinks as a harmless and effete pastime, but in fact it's an evil and insidious force. As evidence of the game's bad influence on child and adult alike, consider this letter written in 1892 by seventeen-year-old Emily Lytton. (She was the granddaughter of the author Edward Bulwer-Lytton, who wrote dozens of bad novels, like *The Last Days of Pompeii*, and began one of them with the phrase that has since become a cliché of atrocious writing, "It was a dark and stormy night . . .").

"After dinner we all played the most exciting game that ever was invented, called Tiddleywinks. . . . I assure you everyone's character changes at Tiddleywinks in the most marvelous way. To begin with, everyone begins to scream at the top of their voices and to accuse everyone else of cheating. . . . Lord Wolmer flicked all the counters off the table and cheated in every possible way. . . . I assure you no words can picture either the intense excitement or the noise."

If the game can do that to refined English aristocrats,

think of the damage it can inflict on impressionable young children from average American families! Perhaps Tipper Gore should forget about putting warning labels on offensive rock 'n' roll albums, and worry about banning tiddlywinks instead.

Who Named the Numbers?

*O*ne, two, three, eleven, twelve, twenty, a hundred, a thou-sand—we take these words for granted. Who invented them? Who decided that *one*, *two*, and so on would represent the numbers they stand for, and why?

With the exception of two numbers, very recently named, no one knows who fabricated these words. Linguists have determined, however, what languages they came from and what changes they went through on their way to becoming standard English. It turns out that our system of naming the numbers isn't much of a system at all. English number words are a hodgepodge, some derived from Latin with roots buried in ancient Sanskrit, others taken directly and more recently from Germanic origins.

It makes sense that the smallest numbers, 1 through 10, have the names with the oldest pedigrees. After all, primitive societies had much more use for the concepts of one, two and three than million, billion, and trillion. All the words for the first ten numbers can be traced back to roots in Sanskrit or the even more ancient proto-Indo-European language. *Four* may be an exception; its ancestry can be traced back to Gothic origins, but researchers are still not sure how or whether it is connected to San-

17

skrit "catvar," from which the romance languages got their words for 4 (French, *quatre*; Spanish, *cuatro*).

The English pronunciations of the very first two numbers have changed in relatively recent times. "One," which comes from Latin *unus* and Greek *oinos*, was originally pronounced "an," then "on," and finally, around the year 1700, "wun." "Two," which is related to the word for 2 in all Indo-European languages, has been pronounced in English as "twah," "twoh," "twoo," and finally "too."

Above 10, the source of the number words shifts from remote Sanskrit to the less ancient Germanic languages. The latter half of both *eleven* and *twelve* comes from the old Teutonic words *leip* or *lif*, meaning "left over." Thus when there were ten of something plus one left over, the quantity was called "one left" (*ein lif*, or eleven); one more than that was "two left" (*twa leip* or *twa lif*, or twelve). After 12, English becomes somewhat more logical for a stretch, giving the numbers 13 through 19 names that suggest "three plus ten," "four plus ten," etc. (French, on the other hand, has idiosyncratic names for not only 11 and 12 but also 13 through 16, before briefly settling down into the equivalent of our teens.)

The words for 20 and other multiples of 10 also have Germanic origins. The suffix "-tig" (which became "-ty") meant "ten." Our "-ty" words today only go as high as "ninety," but in Old English they kept going with what we today might call "tenty," "eleventy," and "twelvety." (The actual Old English word for 110, for example, was "hundendlyftig.") Modern French has departed even farther from consistency; its words for 20, 30, 40, 50, and 60 follow a pattern, but then there's a shift to combinations that require a speaker or listener to perform feats of mental arithmetic: in literal translation, French 70 is "sixty-ten," 80 is "four-twenty," and 90 is "four-twenty-ten."

Hundred is from an old Germanic word, *hund*, meaning 100, and surprisingly, *thousand* seems to be related to it. *Tavas* is the Sanskrit word for "strong," and somehow *ta-*

vas and *hund* may have been put together to mean "a strong hundred" or 1,000. By a similar process, *million* was created in medieval France by putting together *mille* (1,000) and the suffix "-one," which strengthened or amplified the meaning of the word to which it was attached. So *million* means something like "an enlarged thousand."

Billion, trillion, quadrillion, and so on, are derived from *million,* using Greek or Latin words for 2, 3, 4, etc., as prefixes. These large-number words, too, also originated in France, first appearing in the sixteenth century.

The billion-trillion-quadrillion series would seem to be infinitely expandable—just put the next Greek or Latin number together with "-illion" to produce the next number in the sequence. But as science progressed in the nineteenth and twentieth centuries, larger and larger numbers needed to have names. The "-illion" system could conceivably handle them, but the resulting names would be monstrous.

There are two of these large numbers whose names can be credited to a specific individual. The numbers are "googol" and "googolplex," and their names were coined by nine-year-old Milton Sirotta. One day in 1938, Milton was taking a walk with his uncle, mathematician Edward Kasner, who asked him to come up with a name for the number consisting of a 1 followed by one hundred zeros. Kasner promised to use whatever name the child thought up. "Googol," said Milton, who immediately made up a second number name as well: "googolplex," which he originally defined as a 1 followed by as many zeros as you could write before getting tired. Uncle Edward helped him refine the definition to a 1 with a googol of zeros after it, or 10 to the googolth power. Kasner kept his promise and published Milton's names, which are still used by mathematicians today. For example: If you tie a string around this book and hold the other end of the string, how long will it take for the book to jump spontaneously into your hand? That event could occur if, by random chance, enough air molecules happened to hit the book from underneath, while almost none were hitting it from above. Kasner worked out the probabilities and found that if you waited a googolplex of years, the book would almost certainly rise.

In a few cases, English-speaking people can pick from different words (with different histories) for the same number. *Zero* and *cipher* both derive from the Arabic *sifr*, but you can also use *null*, from Latin *ne ullus* (not any). If Germanic "twelve" is not to your liking, you can borrow the Latin *duodecim* (two-ten) and call it a dozen. And if for some reason you don't want to start a sentence with *eighty*, you can use an Old Norse word for "cut" or "notch," harking back to the days when shepherds would cut a notch in a stick for every twenty sheep they counted. Abraham Lincoln did exactly that when he said, "Four-*score* and seven years ago."

Mamas, Don't Let Your Babies Grow Up to Be Slubber Doffers

Still not sure what you want to be when you grow up? Get a copy of the U.S. government's *Dictionary of Occupational Titles*. It lists descriptions of occupations from Abalone Diver and Accordion Tuner to Zanjero and Zyglo Inspector.

It you're a laid-back kind of person, you could become a Groover, a Casual-Shoe Inspector, or a Mellowing-Machine Operator (this last job is in the hat industry). But if you are the more aggressive type, you might want to be a Caustic Operator, a Rough Carpenter, or (the longest job title in the book) a Combat Surveillance and Target Acquisition Non-Commissioned Officer.

Some of these occupations officially recognized by the U.S. government sound downright illegal. But a Reefer Engineer is in charge of refrigeration units on shipboard, not rolling funny cigarettes. A Guillotine Operator cuts pencils, not necks. A White-Kid Buffer isn't guilty of racial discrimination against non-white children who also want to get buffed; he operates a leather buffing machine. A Pusher isn't a drug lord; he's the same as a Straw Boss. And a Liquor Runner doesn't smuggle moonshine past the revenuers; he regulates the flow of syrup in a sugar factory.

Sexy-sounding but disappointing jobs include Bosom

21

Presser (presses blouses in a laundry), Bottom Buffer and Flamer (shoe workers), Chick Sexer (poultry farm), and Top Screw (the boss of a group of cowpunchers). A couple of occupations, though, might really be as exciting as they sound, depending on your tastes: Corset Fitter, Female Impersonator, and Russian Rubber (someone who gives Russian-style massage, not necessarily someone who rubs Russians).

King Maker and Queen Producer sound like jobs for powerful behind-the-scenes politicians, but in fact they are in the candy and beekeeping businesses, respectively. And Bank Boss isn't a job for a Morgan or a Rockefeller; it means either the superintendent of a levee along a river or someone in charge of a group of coal miners.

Napoleon said that an army marches on its stomach, and there is a virtual army of occupations having to do with bellies. Belly Dancer means what it sounds like; Belly Opener, Belly Packer, Belly Trimmer, and Salt-Bellies Overhauler are meat-packing workers; Belly Rollers and Belly Wringers work with leather; and a Belly Builder is not a physical-fitness trainer but someone who makes parts of musical instruments.

Probably the most disgusting-sounding job titles have to do with food processing. You could go into a poultry plant and become a Gizzard-Skin Remover. In a meat-packing plant you could find a Brain Picker and a Hog-Head Singer (not someone who sings about hogs' heads, but someone who singes the hair off them, and removes nose hair from the snout, in preparation for making head-cheese, potted meat food product, etc.—bon appetit!). And no fish cannery would be complete without a Slimer to remove slime from fish.

The choices go on and on. If Pastry Cook isn't specialized enough for you, there's also Psychiatric Hospital Pastry Cook. If Christmas is your favorite time of year, you can be a Santa Claus, a Santa's Helper, or a Reindeer Rancher.

Or you could work in a textile mill and be a Lingo

Cleaner, Pompom Maker, Mangle Doffer, Dobby Looms Pegger, or Slubber Doffer. This last title describes someone who removes, or *doffs*, bobbins of yarn from the spindle of a slubber machine (which, as the government document explains, is a device that "draws out and loosely twists sliver into roving").

And if your mommy doesn't quit pestering you about what you want to be when you grow up, you could always call the phonograph-record factory and ask them to send over a Mother Tester and a Mother Repairer.

Hey! They're Playing *My* Song!

Hᴇᴀʀ ye, hear ye, hear ye! The United States District Court for the Southern District of New York is now in session and will, at great expense to the taxpayers, hear the very important case of "The Cunnilingus Champion of Company C!"

. . . or the case of the nude Mickey Mouse Club, or George Harrison versus the Chiffons, or one of the other famous and not-so-famous lawsuits over song plagiarism. The court will then probably render a decision that does absolutely nothing to clear up the question of where to draw the line between similarity and stealing.

Although it's not possible to state a precise rule regarding song plagiarism, it is possible to say what the rule is *not*. "The superstition among many musicians that the copying of three bars from a musical work can never constitute an infringement is, of course, without foundation," according to the authoritative law textbook *Nimmer on Copyright*. Sometimes you can use the whole tune of somebody else's song and get away with it. In other cases, the similarity of just a few notes is enough to enable the original composer to sue for damages.

A little borrowing is perfectly all right if it's done as part of a parody or satire. The most important precedent was a 1964 suit by songwriters, including Irving Berlin, against *Mad* magazine, which had published humorous lyrics to be sung to the tunes of the plaintiffs' hit songs. *Mad* turned "A Pretty Girl Is Like a Melody" into a story of a hypochondriac, "Louella Schwartz Describes Her Malady," and "The Last Time I Saw Paris" into "The First Time I Saw Maris," poking fun at TV commercials starring baseball player Roger Maris. The court decided that *Mad* was blameless. There was no claim that *Mad* was trying to pass off its lyrics as the actual popular songs or that the verses in *Mad* would diminish public demand for Irving Berlin's originals. Parody and satire, the court ruled, are "independent forms of creative effort . . . worthy of judicial protection in the public interest." A parodist can even directly lift a few lines from the copyrighted original in order to "recall or conjure up" the work being parodied.

The rule was tested again in 1978, when *Saturday Night Live*, the NBC television show, did a skit making fun of the "I Love New York" advertising campaign. The *SNL* sketch depicted a public-relations firm in biblical times thinking up an "I Love Sodom" campaign to rehabilitate the city's naughty image. The words were different, but the tune was the same as "I Love New York." The owner of the song's copyright sued the network and lost. The plaintiff had argued that it might be okay to quote the tune in a parody of the *song* but that the skit was parodying the *city* instead, so the *Mad* magazine precedent did not apply in this case. Maybe so, said the judge, but the ad agency had done such a good job with its campaign that the song was strongly identified with the city, making a parody of one equivalent to a parody of the other. (Congratulations, your campaign was a howling success, so you lose!)

The producers of *Let My People Come* weren't as lucky as NBC. At first glance, it looks as if they followed the same path. The 1974 off-Broadway musical contained a song, "The Cunnilingus Champion of Company C," whose tune was very close to that of "The Boogie-Woogie Bugle Boy of Company B," a 1940 Andrews Sisters hit that had just been revived by Bette Midler. The owners of the copyright to "Bugle Boy" sued and won. The court pointed out that "Champion" wasn't in any way a parody of "Bugle Boy"; and even if it was, much more music was copied than was necessary to "conjure up" the original in the audience's mind.

An even bolder (in more ways than one) case of plagiarism involved Mature Pictures Corp. and its movie *The Life and Times of the Happy Hooker*. In one scene, three male actors, wearing Mickey Mouse hats and nothing else, sing the theme from the Mickey Mouse Club television show, while the starlet services three other men on and around a pool table. The Walt Disney studios were not amused, and filed suit. Mature Pictures argued that the use of the song was a parody that emphasized "the transition . . . from childhood to manhood . . . in a highly comical setting," but the judge didn't swallow it. It's not a parody, he ruled; it's just an out-and-out rip-off of the song. The producers were forbidden to use the song in the movie, and a gag order ensured that Mature Pictures couldn't even use the story of the lawsuit in publicity for the movie. The judge was even-handed, though; he also forbade Disney from using the case as publicity for the Mickey Mouse Club.

(Walt Disney's empire guards its copyrights jealously and often refuses to allow use of its songs and cartoon characters, even when asked permission and offered a fee. In the film *Who's Afraid of Virginia Woolf*, for example, Elizabeth Taylor sings the title song to the tune of "Here We Go 'Round the Mulberry Bush," because Disney refused to allow the tune "Who's Afraid of the Big Bad Wolf" to be used in the movie. Adolf Hitler, by the way, enjoyed "Big Bad Wolf" and was occasionally heard whistling it.)

The rules so far: You can't steal the whole tune of a song unless you're doing a parody, but the *judge* decides what's a parody and what's not. Confusing? Stay tuned, music fans; it gets worse.

If the two songs in question aren't obviously the same, the court must apply the test of "substantial similarity." If the songs are substantially similar *and* if it is proved that the alleged plagiarizer heard or had an opportunity to hear the original song, then the earlier songwriter wins the case.

There are several ways to determine substantial similarity, according to copyright-law expert Russell J. Frackman. The "audience test" asks whether the average reasonable person would think that plagiarism had occurred. The "abstractions test" considers whether two works are the same at some not-very-high level of abstraction. (This is used more in cases of written works than for music, as is the "patterns test," which compares the "sequence of events and development and interplay of characters.") There's also the vague "total-concept-and-feel test," which is becoming important in lawsuits over computer software as well. Finally, there is a "bifurcated test," in which the court must decide whether both the general idea and the specific expression of that idea were stolen.

There you have the rules, but they don't help much. Some more real-life lawsuits, however, might provide a better idea of what constitutes plagiarism.

George Harrison's "My Sweet Lord" and Ronnie Mack's "He's So Fine" (sung by the Chiffons) were the subject of what is probably the most famous song plagiarism case (officially called *Bright Times* v. *Harrisongs*). Beatles fans will be relieved that although George lost the case, the judge emphasized that he didn't *deliberately* steal the tune; the copyright infringement, he said, had been "subconsciously accomplished." George had almost certainly heard "He's So Fine," which was number one on both the American and British charts in 1963, so that settled the question of access. And the songs were substantially similar, according to the judge: the three-note theme is exactly the same, and the four-fold repetition of "really want to see you" has the same tune (including a distinctive grace note) as the corresponding lines in the original song. (In addition to settling the legal issues, by the way, the court's opinion informs us that the gibberish word the Chiffons sing between lines of the song is spelled *dulang*.)

The Belmonts cashed in on the publicity surrounding the case in 1976 by recording their own version of "My Sweet Lord," alternating lines from the lyrics of both songs. Presumably, the Belmonts got all the necessary copyright permissions in advance.

The owners of the 1966 hit "Tiny Bubbles" sued United Artists over some music in the 1969 film *Secret of Santa Vittoria* but lost. The movie's composer, Ernest Gold, claimed he had never heard "Tiny Bubbles." Besides, the judge ruled, the first four notes of the song, which were the crux of this case, are musically commonplace, found in many other tunes, including the chimes of Big Ben and the song "In the Blue Ridge Mountains of Virginia." This was sufficient evidence to allow the jury to conclude that Gold had composed the theme independently of "Tiny Bubbles," and they did just that.

Anheuser-Busch used the same argument in successfully defending itself against a suit by composer Steve Karmen, author of the jingle "When you say Budweiser, you've said it all." Karmen wanted to be paid extra for the use of the similar tune in A-B's new campaign ("For all you do, this Bud's for you"). But the brewery argued, and the judge agreed, that the musical phrase in question (the quarter-note rest and the last four notes) had been used frequently, especially the last two notes. (Two notes? Whoever said "de minimis non curat lex"—the law does not concern itself with small things—had never heard of this case.)

From these and other cases, a rule seems to emerge: A short passage, six or even four notes, is enough to prove "substantial similarity" between two songs. However, the fact that the passage has been used in many other songs is admissible as evidence that the tune could have been composed independently, without plagiarism. And in practice, the shorter the musical phrase, the more likely it is that you can find songs that contain it. Therefore, regardless of the official statements of the law, it's very difficult to win suits over brief snatches of music.

One lawsuit concerned itself not with music but with lyrics—in fact, just one word of the lyrics, although it could hardly be called a brief snatch. The composers of the 1951 song "Supercalafajalistickespeealadojus" sued Walt Disney Productions and Julie Andrews over a song from the film *Mary Poppins*, the somewhat dissimilarly titled "Supercalifragilisticexpialidocious," which had a different tune. (Out of kindness to the court stenographer, the judge announced at the outset that "all variants of this tongue twister will hereinafter be referred to collectively as 'the word.' ") Plaintiff Barney Young argued that he had invented the word as a child in 1921. His song was not published until thirty years later, and by then, ruled the judge, other people knew the word, so it was therefore in the public domain. Julie Andrews could legally sing it, even if she wasn't very good at spelling it.

Repetition, Repetition, Repetition, Repetition— Huh?

IT's happened to you before, and you can easily make it happen again. A word, a good, ancient, English word, that has served millions of people in conveying meaning loses its meaning for you simply because you repeat it over and over to yourself. Try it. Pick a word, any word: *loses*, for example. Say it now. Then say it over and over, forty or fifty times: Loses. Loses. Loses. Loses. Loses. Loses . . .

Used to mean something, didn't it? And now it sounds like a word from Albanian or Zulu or Martian.

Don't worry: Not only is this a common experience, but the phenomenon has been studied by scientists for almost a century (that's another good one: century, century, century, century, century, century . . .). Researchers have given it the name "semantic satiation," and there are several theories about why it happens.

Psychologists at Barnard College in New York made the first known attempt to investigate this effect in 1907. Instead of repeating a word over and over, they asked people to stare at a six-letter word for three minutes and describe the changes that seemed to occur in its meaning. For example, with the word *rumble*, one subject said that at first it reminded her of the sound of thunder, then of the sound of a bumble bee. After twenty-one seconds, it seemed to divide into two parts, *rum* and *ble*. After a minute, it called to mind Charles Dickens's character Uriah Heep, who often used the word *'umble*. After eighty-one seconds, the word had no meaning at all. After two and a half minutes, the subject said she could think of the sound, but it no longer bore any relation to the look of the word. After three minutes, she said the letters themselves looked "queer."

The researchers admitted there were some problems with the design of their experiment. For one thing, the subjects were all people (apparently psychology students) with a "fair amount of introspective training," not a representative sample of the population. Furthermore, the experiment involved staring at a printed word, not repeating it over and over, so it didn't address the question of why *saying* a word repeatedly produces the satiation effect. The researchers did, however, speculate on how a word loses its meaning following long visual exposure. Perhaps, they suggested, the meaning may disappear when the sound of the word becomes overwhelmed by, and therefore separated from, its look and spelling. Or maybe after staring at a word for a while the mind separates it symmetrically, turning *mother* or *caught* into the confusing configurations *mot-her* and *cau-ght*. (A later researcher has proposed that the *sound* of a word may actually be perceived differently after many voiced repetitions just as its *look* may appear to change after long fixation.)

The 1907 study also put forward another possibility, the hypnosis hypothesis: Perhaps the subject's concentration narrows to exactly one thing—the look or sound of the word—as in hypnosis, or meditation on a mantra, and all connections between the word and its meaning get lost. A more recent experiment bolstered the hypnosis theory. People who merely repeated the word *push* over and over reported loss of meaning sooner than people who were told to push in a dresser drawer with each repetition. Because the second group had an action to associate with the word, they may have been able to connect the word with the meaning longer than those who simply repeated "push, push, push." It took about forty repetitions, on the average, for the word to become gibberish to the subjects who were only repeating the word.

Another way to test the hypnosis hypothesis might be to compare what happens to words like *green* or *elephant*, with which the subject can associate a picture, versus abstract words like *honest* or *useful*. (The words chosen should probably have similar attributes, such as an equal number of letters or syllables, and constitute the same part of speech, e.g., all verbs or all nouns, to prevent extraneous differences from affecting the outcome.) Presumably, the abstract words would turn to nonsense before the concrete terms. Apparently, no such experiment has been conducted.

The experiments that have been done shared one defect: The scientists told the subjects beforehand exactly what they were looking for. This may have biased the results, since the subjects may have reported loss of meaning even when it didn't actually occur, because they wanted to meet the researchers' expectations. To overcome this problem, one psychologist has suggested repeating a word over and over to one group of subjects but not to another (the control group), and then asking each participant to choose a word of similar meaning from a list—without telling them beforehand what's being studied. This experiment also remains untried.

Semantic satiation theories abound, but none is confirmed. So for all you current and future psychology majors out there, here's a good topic for your thesis, thesis, thesis, thesis, thesis, thesis . . .

Rat Writs

THE lawyer was Bartholomew Chassenee, the court was a church tribunal, the place was France, the year was 1520, and the defendants were rats.

The defendants were charged with destroying crops on farm after farm. Because they had no attorney, the court appointed Chassenee to represent them, and a clever tactician he turned out to be. First, he objected to the trial on the grounds that the summons had not been correctly served on all the defendants. The court agreed, and ordered it to be read publicly in all the churches of all the parishes where the accused rats resided. Once that technicality was taken care of, Chassenee delayed the trial again by arguing that his clients could not safely come to defend themselves because on the way, they might be eaten by cats.

Animals, and even inanimate objects, have been prosecuted in societies all over the world from ancient times onward, but medieval Europeans seem to have been the world champions at the practice. Both church and secular courts heard charges against individual pigs, cattle, and horses, and even whole species of insects. They imposed a broad range of punishments, including the death penalty, but they also granted the animals an abundance of rights and legal protection.

33

The church courts dealt mostly with vermin rather than with domestic animals. Insects, rats, and such were tried as a class or species and, if convicted, were anathematized (officially cursed). Sometimes a few individuals would be executed, too, to set an example.

These courts had to decide the touchy question of whether the pests were agents of the devil—in which case the church would try to drive them away with incantations—or agents of God sent to warn or chastise His erring flock—in which case the church would counsel the people to mend their ways, and urge the creatures to leave once their mission was accomplished.

The authorities often proclaimed that the vermin would be more likely to vanish if people would remember to give their tithes to the church. They cited the biblical Book of Malachi: "Bring me all the tithes into the storehouse . . . saith the Lord . . . and I will rebuke the devourer for your sakes, and he shall not destroy the fruits of your ground."

In any event, the church was in a no-lose situation. If the ravaging hordes ceased their destructive activities, the church took credit for the success of its legal proceedings against the offenders; and if not, it was the fault of the congregation's persistence in wicked ways.

Domestic animals, on the other hand, were treated as individuals and tried like people. Pigs figure most often in these old European trials; during the Middle Ages they were often allowed to run free, endangering children in particular. Many pigs were executed for eating babies, but one was judged guiltier than usual, because it scarfed up a child on a Friday—a day on which, by decree of the church, the consumption of meat was forbidden.

Animals were *prosecuted* as if they were humans, but they were also afforded the same legal rights in court. The rats' lawyer, Chassenee, later became a judge and used the rat precedent to protect some accused Waldensian heretics, who emulated the poverty of Christ and questioned church teachings on predestination, justification by faith, and the sacraments. The prosecution didn't want the heretics to be represented by counsel, but Chassenee reasoned that if rats could have an attorney, so could human defendants. Chassenee died before the trial got under way, though, and the heretics wound up without legal representation after all. In another French case, in 1750, a man and a mare were accused of bestiality. Often, both man and animal were executed in such cases, but on this occasion the horse was acquitted on the grounds that she had not consented to the act.

These old animal cases foreshadowed various twentieth-century issues of human justice. Today, groups like Amnesty International protest against punishment without trial, but so did the citizens of Schweinfurt, Germany, in 1576. When the city executioner killed a pig accused of murder (but not yet tried), an angry mob ran him out of town.

The sorry history of Europeans dispossessing American Indians of their land also has a parallel in the animal cases. Termites were devouring the food and furniture of a Brazilian monastery in 1713. The monks sued the termites, but the critters' lawyer argued that, having settled there first, they had rights which superseded the monastery's. He also noted pointedly that the termites were much more industrious and productive than the monks. The court, in a "compromise" verdict, ordered the original inhabitants to remove themselves to some land that would be set aside where they could live undisturbed—in other words, a bug reservation. The official church historian who recorded the trial asserted that the termites obeyed the court and marched out of the monastery in orderly columns.

Historian Leon Menebrea, writing in 1846, suggested that the prosecution of animals under human and divine law, with all its faults, was still a step forward toward respect for all creatures. Nonsense, wrote E. P. Evans, another expert on the subject, in 1906; it was the product of a society "in which dense ignorance was governed by brute force."

Has there really been much progress since the Middle Ages? Similar prosecutions have occurred even in relatively recent times. Insects were tried in Denmark in 1805 and in Slavonia (present-day Yugoslavia) in 1866. A pig was executed in Slavonia in 1864 for biting off a child's ears, and animals were routinely executed for murder in some central African societies during the nineteenth century. Fifteen wooden statues that had fallen on a man and killed him were beheaded in China around 1900.

Even today, and especially in America, the social distinction between people and animals is often blurred. As J. J. Finkelstein, yet another expert on animal justice, has pointed out, we now have pet food, pet motels, pet schools (complete with diplomas), and pet cemeteries—and our society continues to prosecute animals in court. The defendant is usually a dog these days, and although such cases aren't officially titled *People of the State of California* v. *Fido*, it's still the *dog's* life, not the owner's, that is at stake.

In recent times there has been some undoing of the injustices of those old tribunals. A bell, which had been sent to Siberia for signaling a rebellion in 1591, was pardoned and returned home three hundred years later. And—by way of poetic justice—we will never know the outcome of a 1587 trial of worms in the Bordeaux wine country, because the last page of the only existing copy of the trial transcript has been eaten. By worms.

Crude, Lewd, and Eschewed Food

IT's getting harder and harder to make a list of repulsive things that "they" eat but "we" don't. Blackened elk chops, alligator étouffée, and chamois with wild mushroom sauce are on the menu at Henry's End restaurant in Brooklyn, and the chef at Yamazushi in Durham, North Carolina, will try to serve you something that grosses out even many confirmed sushi fans: meat cut from a living lobster.

Fried grubs (Mexico), live shrimp (Hunan, China), dormouse (ancient Rome), and fox (nineteenth-century Russia), though, are among the delicacies of other times and places that have not yet made it onto McDonald's menu of Yankee Doodle favorites. And those are some of the *least* disgusting things that our fellow humans have decided are tasty.

In Paris—the world capital of food snobbery—horse meat was all the rage in the 1870s. (Parisians started eating it during the Franco-Prussian war, when beef was unavailable, and discovered they liked it.) Scots are fiercely proud of their haggis—a sheep's stomach, filled with minced lungs, hearts, and other entrails and boiled to perfection. The ancient Egyptians liked elephant so much that the pharaohs had to enact one of the world's first environmental regulations to prevent them from being hunted to extinction. The ancient Greeks ate dog, as do modern Koreans and some Chinese, although many Chinese find the idea repugnant.

But leave it to the gluttonous, decadent ancient Romans to win the prize for eating the most repulsive foods ever.

Nowadays, Romans eat a lot of pasta, but in ancient times nearly every Roman recipe called for at least a dash of *garum*. The word comes from the Greek *garos*, meaning "shrimp"; so far, so good. But *garum* was shrimp, or other fish, prepared in a special way: fish, preferably the entrails, mixed with salt and allowed to putrify, then mixed with wine or vinegar and left uncovered for two or three months.

One favorite Roman food was the lubridan, or sea wolf, a kind of fish. Most lubridans cost about the same as other fish, but those caught between two particular bridges in Rome were astronomically expensive. That part of the Tiber River happened to be where the city sewers dumped their raw offal. These fish that fed on filth were sought out by wealthy Roman families, such as those of Julius Caesar and Lucullus (whose name comes down to us in the phrase "Lucullan feast," meaning a meal at which the guests eat their fill, deliberately vomit, then return for more).

The favorite dish of the first-century Roman emperor Vitellius came, not from the sewers of Rome, but from the far reaches of the Roman Empire. Naval vessels brought him (at public expense, of course) the ingredients of the meal he called "the shield of Minerva": pike-fish livers, peacock and pheasant brains, flamingo tongues, and the gonads of lampreys.

The foods *we* consider expensive delicacies may well be cheap cat food in future centuries, and vice versa. Consider the poor oppressed servants in wealthy Scotsmen's castles three hundred years ago. They were given the same food so often that they finally refused to accept it more than five times a week. The disgusting stuff that was being forced down their throats? Fresh Scottish salmon.

The Fate of the Moon

WILL the moon ever fall into the earth, like a tired Sputnik or Skylab? No—and yes—and no.

Astronomers think they have the answer to that question now, but finding it was not easy. Calculating the future of the moon's orbit is like "playing chess in three dimensions—blindfolded," said mathematician E. W. Brown. He published his three-volume tables of the lunar orbit in 1919, but even with today's supercomputers, the prediction of the moon's position is not an exact science.

The moon and the earth, unlike those imaginary planets on a freshman physics exam, are not perfectly round; their irregularity makes the calculation harder. And you have to factor in the gravity of the sun and the planets, whose motions are themselves not precisely known. And so on.

One of the forces confusing the calculation is the friction caused by the tides. (Lunar gravity creates tides not only in the oceans but also the dry land, which moves up and down several inches twice a day.) Tidal friction slows the earth's rotation, making our "day" one second longer every 120,000 years. And as the earth slows down, the moon must move farther away, according to the laws of physics, to preserve the angular momentum of the earth/moon system.

Eventually, the "day" and the "month" will become the same length, and one side of each celestial body will

39

face the other body at all times. The earth and moon will then be 340,000 miles apart, as compared to 240,000 miles today.

Then, with the earth and moon no longer inflicting changing tides on each other, the *sun's* tidal forces will become more significant, causing the earth and moon to move closer again. Finally, the moon will come so close to the earth—12,000 miles—that it will break up into little pieces and form rings like Saturn's.

This, or something like it, *would* happen if there were enough time. But the whole process would take tens of billions of years. Before that happens, the sun will have died, taking the earth and moon with it. So the sky *is* falling, but that's the least of earth's worries.

What ™ Are ® These sm?

PEOPLE in TV commercials don't talk like real people. No one would ever say, "Have some Sanka *brand* decaffeinated coffee!" But lawyers make the actors speak that way to keep the word *Sanka* from losing its status as a trademark and becoming a common word, as Bayer's *aspirin* did years ago.

The first trademarks appeared in Europe sometime before the year 1300. Some were derived from ancient runic alphabets, while others were pictures of the product, or arbitrary symbols. They were useful in international shipping, because dockworkers and merchants who didn't speak foreign languages could nevertheless recognize a foreign seller's mark. Medieval aristocrats didn't like the idea of trademarks because it looked to them as if upstart middle-class merchants were trying to muscle in on the aristocracy's monopoly on coats of arms.

Today trademarks are everywhere, identified by millions of intrusive little TM and ® symbols. Both symbols mean that someone is claiming ownership of a trademark and prohibiting anyone else from using it without permission. The first person or company to put a product into commerce and identify it by certain words or pictures owns that identifying trademark, and can use the TM symbol to

41

protect it. (If the mark identifies a service instead of a product, it's a service mark, or SM, instead.)

If the trademark owner wants to go to the additional trouble and expense—and get the additional benefits—he can register the mark with the U.S. Patent Office, and use ® or "Reg. U.S. Patent Office" rather than TM or SM. Registration provides certain legal advantages: The burden of proof as to trademark ownership is on the challenger, not the registered owner; the courts will "construe notice" (that is, they will assume that the challenger knew about the registration of the trademark, even if he really didn't); and the owner can collect triple damages for any infringement. But registration of a trademark doesn't guarantee ownership. If a challenger can prove he used and owned the trademark first, he can take away the registered owner's precious little ®.

Sometimes it seems that the trademark lawyers won't rest until they've trademarked every single word in the language. Already "United Way," "The Supremes," and "Captain Kangaroo" are registered trademarks. Even an unlikely champion of private property, the communist magazine *New Masses*, printed this copyright and trademark notice in every issue: "Copyright 1935, New Masses, Inc. *Reg. U.S. Pat. Off.* Drawings and text may not be reprinted without permission." (Maybe they meant "Registered Trade Marx.")

Black Rod and the Highway Robbers

GREAT Britain, that "sceptered isle," is full of royalty and nobility and titles and class distinctions. Many of its traditions stem from a time when the king and his lords were unquestioned masters and the common people had no rights.

But there are some British traditions that symbolize more recent and more democratic values. Of course, Britain being Britain, even these democratic customs are sometimes quaint and bizarre. Two of them—slamming the door in Black Rod's face and the introduction of the Outlawries Bill—take place at the ceremonial opening of each session of Parliament.

The queen officially opens Parliament by giving a speech in the House of Lords. When she arrives there, she summons the members of the House of Commons to come hear the speech. Her summons is delivered by an official called the Gentleman Usher of the Black Rod, or just Black Rod for short.

(Black Rod is actually in charge of security for the House of Lords; the job is traditionally given as a reward to a retired military officer. The title refers to the ceremonial ebony staff he carries on official occasions.)

Black Rod walks across the palace of Westminster to deliver the royal summons to the Commons. But as he approaches, the door to the Commons chamber is slammed in his face and is not opened until he knocks three times with his black rod and receives permission to enter. This symbolizes the right of the House of Commons to meet without royal interference.

After hearing the queen's speech (which is actually written by the prime minister and outlines the government's legislative plans for the upcoming session), the members of the Commons return to their chamber to consider the speech. But just before that order of business, someone introduces a bill. The title of this bill is always the same: "A bill for the more effectual preventing [of] clandestine outlawries." The so-called Outlawries Bill has no text, and is introduced solely to demonstrate that Parliament has the right to conduct whatever business it pleases, and is not required to consider the queen's speech as the first item.

Because the Outlawries Bill is purely symbolic, it is never actually debated—well, almost never. In 1946, two Conservative members tried to speak on the bill as a publicity stunt attacking labor unions. One of them said that although the original form of "outlawry" the bill was intended to prevent—highway robbery—had disappeared, "there are many other forms of outlawry, especially the closed [union] shop." Mr. Speaker ruled the debate out of order, and the House went on to consider the royal speech as usual.

The Woman Who Will Never Die

HUMAN placental blood, ground-up cow fetus, plasma from blood extracted from the hearts of living chickens. Sounds like the contents of a witches' cauldron. But this isn't a ghost story. Not really. Not even though it involves a thirty-one-year-old mother of four named Henrietta Lacks who died in 1951, but who has been showing up ever since, as a welcome guest and as an uninvited trespasser in laboratories around the world, and even in outer space.

It isn't really Mrs. Lacks herself who appears posthumously; it's some of her cells that were kept alive after her death. That is, some descendants of the cells from the cancer that killed her.

In 1951, the science of cell culture was in its infancy. George and Margaret Gey, researchers at Johns Hopkins University hospital in Baltimore, had been having some success keeping cells from cancerous tumors alive and multiplying by bathing them in a solution containing the sinister-sounding ingredients mentioned earlier. (They got the plasma by going out to a helpful chicken farmer's place early in the morning and jabbing hypodermic needles into the living birds' hearts. Many of the chickens survived, but whenever one didn't, the Geys would buy it from the farmer and have it for dinner that evening.)

45

The Geys had been able to keep human cancer cells alive for weeks and even months in the lab, but eventually the cultures lost strength and died off.

One day in 1951 the Geys removed a tumor from a body in the morgue—Mrs. Lacks's body. Her cancer, which killed her more quickly than her doctors had expected, grew ten to twenty times faster than other cultured cells, and never gave up and died as other cancer cells did.

Following standard procedure in the scientific community, this "line" of cells grown from Mrs. Lacks's cancer was named using the first two letters of the first and last names of its donor: HeLa cells (pronounced hey-lah). Many medical researchers jumped at the opportunity to use these cells in their studies because of their ability to survive long journeys through the mail and long storage and use in the lab. After the development of orbiting satellites, the cells were even launched into space for research on the effect of weightlessness on cancer.

Cell culture soon became a big business—and a confusing one, thanks to HeLa. Mrs. Lacks's cancer cells were so tenacious and aggressive that they took over other cell cultures in some labs where sloppy procedures were used. Even in research facilities with more careful technicians, HeLa cells sometimes floated through the air and began growing in the wrong Petri dishes. It got to the point where cultures labeled and sold as "healthy monkey" or "male human" were actually derived from the cancer of Henrietta Lacks.

Cancer researchers actually came to some terribly wrong conclusions before HeLa's aggressiveness became known. Paper after paper was published in scholarly journals showing that all forms of cancer had various traits in common, when in fact all the "different" cancers the doctors had been studying were only one cancer, that of Mrs. Lacks.

By the 1970s, some researchers had discovered that many supposedly different cell lines were really HeLa, including some grandiosely donated to American doctors by their Soviet colleagues. The discoverers of this fact, however, were not exactly thanked by their fellow scientists. They were, instead, loudly criticized and spurned by other researchers, whose work had been called into question by the discovery. Although the spread of HeLa was eventually accepted as an unfortunate fact, those who found it out were not quickly made heroes of medicine. At least one had to retire early when the government cut off funding for his lab.

The Straight Poop on Dogs

• Dead dogs in many cities are sent to a plant that renders them into protein supplements for hogs and chickens. The leftover grease is used to make soap. "This," said ecologist Alan Beck, a former New York City health official, "is one of the few examples of recycling natural components in the urban environment."

• Dogs deposited an estimated five to twenty thousand tons of feces onto the sidewalks of New York each year before the clean-up-after-your-dog law was enacted. Even with that law, those kilotons of deep doodoo have to go somewhere, and as any New Yorker knows, not all of it is picked up by yuppie puppy owners with plastic gloves and Pooper Scooper shovels. And the law says nothing about the million gallons of dog urine emitted annually, all of which goes down the storm drains or into the soil of city parks.

• Each instance of dog excrement not scooped up eventually yields, on the average, 144 flies.

• Dog urine is a significant threat to a city's environment. It kills tree bark on contact and adds salt to the soil. These effects kill trees, which, had they lived, could have reduced noise and pollution.

• The first clean-up-after-your-dog law was enacted in Nutley, New Jersey, in 1971.

• If your favorite dog food says it contains "meat by-products," then, by law, it may be made from the lungs, livers, spleens, kidneys, and "intestines (free from their contents)" of cattle, swine, sheep, and goats. But at least it can't contain skin, horns, teeth, or hooves without mentioning them on the label.

• That cute puppy you gave your kids could blind them. Children are especially susceptible to VLM (visceral larva migrans), a tiny worm that infects dogs and related animals and can cause blindness in humans. Animals can get VLM from eating road kills; puppies can inherit it from their mothers. Human children can pick it up by playing with puppies, eating dirt in which dogs have left their calling cards, and even breathing dust from dried dog excrement.

The Rockets' Red Glare and a Risible Phiz

Many Americans know that their national anthem is set to the tune of an old English drinking song named "To Anacreon in Heaven." But few know the original words to the old song.

Now, don't get your hopes up. Because it's described as a drinking song, you might assume that its words are bawdy or uproariously funny or both. Unfortunately, it's not bawdy at all, and even after you've figured out what all the allusions to ancient Greek gods mean, it's only mildly amusing. There's really more action in "The Star-Spangled Banner," which is full of bombs and blood and vengeance.

The music was written around 1780, by J. Stafford Smith, and Ralph Tomlinson wrote the "Anacreon" words. It was the song of the Anacreontic Society, "a jovial musical society for singing choral and part-music, catches, canons, and so on," which met at London's Crown and Anchor tavern in the late eighteenth century.

Before Francis Scott Key wrote the "Star-Spangled Banner" words, American poet Robert Treat Paine had written at least two other poems to the "Anacreon" tune: "Adams and Liberty," in praise of President John Adams, and "Spain," in support of that country's resistance to Napoleon.

But without further ado, here are the *real* words to our national anthem. If you plan to sing it before the next baseball game, note that the name "Anacreon" (he was a Greek poet, circa 500 B.C., who wrote about love and wine) is pronounced an-AK-reon, with the last two syllables pronounced as one in order to fit the song's meter.

To Anacreon in heaven, where he sat in full glee,
A few sons of Harmony sent a petition,
That he their inspirer and patron would be,
When this answer arrived from the jolly old Grecian:
"Voice, fiddle, and flute,
No longer be mute,
I'll lend ye my name, and inspire ye to boot.
And besides, I'll instruct you, like me, to entwine
The myrtle of Venus with Bacchus's vine."

The news through Olympus immediately flew;
When old Thunder pretended to give himself airs—
"If these mortals are suffered their scheme to pursue,
The devil a goddess will stay above stairs.
Hark! already they cry,
In transports of joy,
Away to the Sons of Anacreon we'll fly,
And there, with good fellows, we'll learn to entwine
The myrtle of Venus with Bacchus's vine."

"The yellow hair'd god and his nine fusty maids,
From Helicon's banks will incontinent flee;
Idalia will boast of but tenantless shades,
And the biforked hill a mere desert will be;
My thunder, no fear on't,
Shall soon do its errand,
And damn me, I'll swing the ringleaders, I warrant;
I'll trim the young dogs, for thus daring to twine
The myrtle of Venus with Bacchus's vine."

Apollo rose up and said "Pr'ythee ne'er quarrel,
Good king of the gods, with my votaries below;

Your thunder is useless;"—then, showing his laurel,
Cried *"Sic evitabile fulmen*, you know!
Then over each head
My laurel I'll spread,
So my sons from your crackers no mischief will dread,
Whilst snug in their club-room they jovially twine
The myrtle of Venus with Bacchus's vine."

Next Momus got up, with his risible phiz,
And swore with Apollo he'd cheerfully join—
"The full tide of harmony still shall be his,
But the song, and the catch, and the laugh shall be mine.
Then Jove, be not jealous,
Of these honest fellows."
Cried Jove, "We relent, since the truth you now tell us;
And swear, by old Styx, that they long shall entwine
The myrtle of Venus with Bacchus's vine."

Ye sons of Anacreon, then join hand in hand;
Preserve unanimity, friendship and love.
'Tis yours to support what's so happily planned;
You've the sanction of gods and the fiat of Jove.
While thus we agree,
Our toast let it be—
"May our club flourish happy, united, and free,
And long may the Sons of Anacreon entwine
The myrtle of Venus with Bacchus's vine."

Take Two Leeches and Call Me in the Morning

For centuries, doctors loved leeches. By the 1800s, they had developed an intricate science of using the blood-sucking worms to bleed, and allegedly cure, the sick. Today we laugh at the quaint practice, but the leeches may have the last laugh.

People have used *leech* as a slang term for *doctor* for over a thousand years, which suggests that the practice of leeching patients is even older. The oldest known medical book written in England is the Anglo-Saxon *Leech Book*, written by a doctor named Bald; it dealt with herbal remedies and other medical topics.

No one knows where the idea of bleeding with leeches originated. Medical historians suggest that in ancient times, people may have noticed that women naturally menstruate with no ill effects and from that may have gotten the idea that blood carries away harmful matter from the body.

By 1831, leeches were all the rage. That year, to keep his colleagues up to date on the latest advances in medicine, South Carolina doctor Josiah Nott published his translation of a French book on "the new medical doctrine" of F.J.V. Broussais. At the end, he added his own chapter on the "manner of keeping and using leeches, etc.," because doctors in the backward South (unlike their more sophisticated Yankee and European colleagues) were not familiar with the latest leech technology.

In those days, doctors couldn't just order leeches from a medical supply company, so Nott had to explain how to catch them and keep them alive until a patient needed them. Gathering leeches was easy. Just get some "boys" (by which Nott meant slaves) to roll up their trouser cuffs and walk through a muddy pond; they should emerge with several leeches hanging on to their legs. A doctor who didn't happen to have any "boys" handy could spread a fresh animal skin on the water, raw side down, and wait until the leeches attached themselves to it.

To keep the leeches happy and healthy until mealtime, the doctor needed a wooden tub (Nott suggested using a whiskey barrel sawed in half). The tub, Nott emphasized, must be "perfectly clean"—but should then be filled with water, mud, and marsh grass, because "if this be neglected, they become sickly."

Before using the leeches, the doctor had to wash the area of the patient's skin where they were to be applied, because human odor is "offensive" to the poor little creatures. Once a leech bit and started sucking blood, it had to be left on until it dropped off (about half an hour). If it was pulled off before finishing its meal, it might leave its teeth in the patient.

After a leech has sucked its fill of blood, it can live for a month before it's hungry again. So Nott recommended extracting blood from a leech as soon as possible, so it could be used again in a week or two. The doctor can empty the leech by soaking it in dark beer, which makes it puke, or by making an incision in its tail and dragging out a dollop of partially clotted blood.

American leeches are smaller than their European cousins, so Nott was careful to point out that American doctors might have to double or triple the recipes found in European medical books. He recommended using as many as a hundred leeches to treat serious diseases like encephalitis or pleurisy ("when it is important to make a prompt and decided impression").

Even Nott and his leech-happy hero Broussais didn't believe that leeches were useful in treating all diseases. They are good mainly for inflammations of membranes, such as meningitis. If a spleen, liver, or other organ is itself diseased, Nott recommended venesection or "general bleeding"—large-scale bloodletting from a vein—instead.

Nott admitted that doctors did not understand the differences between blood circulation in the capillaries (where leeches were used) and in the arteries and veins (where general bleeding took place). But he claimed to have observed many times in his own practice that leeching worked where general bleeding did not.

For the doctor whose patient had a problem that leeches could help, Nott had a detailed list of places where the leeches should be applied: for meningitis, the head; for stomach inflammation, the abdomen; for problems of the lower intestine, the anus; for diseases of the genito-urinary tract, there was a wide range of choices, depending on the gender of the patient: the root of the penis, the scrotum, the labia, or the "neck of uterus, &c."

The cures begin to sound worse than the disease. But at least in the case of eye irritations Nott was kinder to his patients than some other doctors, who put leeches on the eyelids and even the conjunctiva (the red membranes under the lids). Nott recommended the neck or temples instead.

Despite his hard work and helpful hints, Nott's timing was awful. He brought out his book just in time to see its theories abandoned. The English doctor Marshall Hall had just published his research on the true function of the capillaries and his attacks on the practice of bloodletting. Then in 1832, a year after Nott's book was published, his mentor Broussais's methods were abandoned in France when leeches failed to stop a cholera epidemic there.

There the matter lay for 150 years. But in the 1980s, researchers discovered that the old-time "leeches" may have been right after all in attributing their cures to the sucking worms. It turns out that leech saliva contains substances that keep blood flowing freely (anticoagulants and vasodilators) as well as antibiotics and a local anesthetic. These chemicals are useful in research on afflictions as diverse as heart attacks, arthritis, and glaucoma.

Nowadays, the leech's contribution to medicine isn't just chemicals, test tubes, and lab work. Dr. Felix Freshwater, chief surgeon at Cedars Medical Center in Miami, uses real live leeches to help restore the blood flow to reattached severed fingers and ears. They cost $6 each from Biopharm, Ltd., a British leechmonger, which sold fifty thousand of the worms in 1989.

If you're offered leech treatment the next time you visit your doctor, don't panic. In fact, count your blessings. At least you'll have upscale scars, because leech bites look just like the three-pointed Mercedes-Benz logo. Besides, you *could* do worse: researchers have discovered that some of the same pharmacologically active chemicals found in leeches are also present in the saliva of vampire bats.

Patron Saints

WHATEVER your occupation, it probably has its own patron saint. But few professions are as blessed as that noble and ancient calling—*public relations*? Yes, not only does the P.R. profession as a whole have a patron, St. Bernardine of Siena, a preacher who lived around 1400, but those who do P.R. for hospitals have a more specialized patron, St. Paul the Apostle.

Several other saints are patrons of modern professions as well: St. Francis of Assisi for ecologists; the Archangel Gabriel, God's messenger, for TV workers; and the Archangel Michael, captain of the heavenly host, for paratroopers. (Saints don't have to be human—the archangels are saints too.)

Many age-old professions also have patron saints, who are probably not as busy these days as they once were. Chandlers (candle makers) pray to St. Ambrose, a fourth-century liturgist who developed a style of singing called Ambrosian chant, and who promoted the use of candles in church services. St. Cloud, a sixth-century king turned monk, is the patron of nail makers.

Some patron saints' duties are easy to guess. St. Bernard of Menthon, who built way stations for medieval travelers in the Alps, and after whom the dog breed is named, is the patron of mountain climbers. (Coincidentally, the saying "Love me, love my dog" was coined by St. Bernard of Clairvaux, who lived almost a century later, and had nothing to do with Alpine travelers.) St. Vitus is the patron of people who suffer from epilepsy (which used to be called "St. Vitus's dance")—and also of comedians, an assignment that probably comes from less enlightened times, when seizures were considered funny.

Finally, there are two saints who have made it big in the world of entertainment. St. Elmo (also called Ermo, Erasmus, or Rasmus) is believed to help those with intestinal disorders, so you might think that "St. Elmo's Fire," in addition to being the name of a movie, refers to heartburn. In fact, it's the name given to a natural electrical discharge often seen emanating from ships at sea. The "fire" was so named by sailors, who are also under St. Elmo's protection. And St. Eligius, whose name was given to the hospital in the TV show *St. Elsewhere*, was a seventh-century French goldsmith and government official who is the patron saint of metalworkers.

(*St. Elsewhere* actually comes from the name Mount Saint Elsewhere, a slang expression used in the medical community to mean a typical mediocre hospital. The phrase was popularized in Dr. Samuel Shem's hilarious novel about interns, *The House of God*.)

Citizen's Arrest

WHAT'S wrong with this picture: "Hello, Mr. Jones, this is the police. Would you please come arrest a drunk driver for us?" Isn't that backward? Shouldn't Mr. Jones be calling the cops, not vice versa? Welcome to the confusing world of citizen's arrest!

A man driving on a highway in Covina, California, in 1977, saw another car weaving in and out of traffic, sometimes even driving in the wrong lane. He followed the car until it turned into a driveway, then went home and called the police. When the officers arrived at the address he had given them, they found a woman slumped over the steering wheel. Apparently, she had passed out just after getting home. But the police hadn't seen her commit any crime: There was nothing illegal about being drunk and unconscious in a stopped car on her own property. The police were powerless to arrest her. So they phoned the man who'd observed her erratic driving, gave him step-by-step instructions on making a valid citizen's arrest, stood by while he carried it out, and then immediately carried *her* out. A court ruled that the whole charade was perfectly legal.

In most cases, though, making a citizen's arrest is dangerous, not just because the suspect might become violent but because of what might happen later, in the courtroom, to the arresting citizen. There are very strict rules governing the conduct of a citizen's arrest, and the laws vary greatly from state to state.

The general common-law rule is that you can legally arrest someone for a felony, provided that the alleged felony actually *did* occur and that you either witnessed the crime or have reasonable grounds for believing that the suspect was the person who committed it. (Notice the pitfall here: If you *think* that the suspect committed the crime but in fact no such crime was committed by anyone, the citizen's arrest is illegal and you're in trouble.) You can also arrest someone for "affray or breach of the peace"— that is, a misdemeanor committed in public, not on private property—but only if it was committed in your presence. (Another pitfall: You have to know which crimes are felonies and which are misdemeanors.) Many states have passed laws that complicate the matter even further.

The general common *sense* rule is: Don't make a citizen's arrest. Here are the sad tales of a couple of people who didn't follow that rule. Both lost a lot of money, and one was seriously wounded as well.

When Detroit was putting up its first electric streetlights in 1884, the power company erected a pole near the home of a Mr. Ross and guyed it to a post in Ross's lawn. Ross didn't like that and sawed off the post. The president of the power company, on learning of this act of disrespect toward his great institution, went to Ross's house, arrested him, and took him down to the police superintendent's home, where he was held for four hours. A criminal court later acquitted him of vandalism, and Ross turned around and successfully sued the electric company's president. The civil court found the citizen's arrest illegal because the alleged crime had been a *misdemeanor* and the company president had not personally witnessed it. History does not record whether Ross succeeded in getting the light pole moved away from his house, but his award of $4,500, a very sizable sum in those days, probably helped him recover from his distress over the desecration of his lawn.

Our second citizen's arrest story begins on a hot, sticky Mississippi summer evening in 1967. Therrall Spears, a salesman, was walking across the parking lot of a fast-food joint when a pickup truck nearly hit him. The driver swerved, but then (in the words of the judge who eventually had to unravel this case) gave Spears "an invitation to 'go to hell.' " Spears jumped into his car, gave chase to the pickup for a while, then stopped and tried to call the sheriff but couldn't reach him. After driving around a bit, Spears spotted the pickup parked outside a house. According to the court records, he went to the door brandishing a gun, announced that he was there to make a citizen's arrest, forced his way inside—and was shot by the homeowner.

Spears's insurance company refused to pay his $4,751 medical bill, citing a clause in his policy excluding injuries suffered while committing a felony. Spears countered that his actions constituted a legal citizen's arrest. The state supreme court disagreed, because the driver's alleged misdemeanor had ended long before the attempted arrest. Having broken off the chase (when he tried to call the sheriff), Spears had forfeited the right to make a citizen's arrest under Mississippi law, and ended up not only wounded but also holding the bag for his doctor bills.

Apparently, taking a bite out of crime can also take a bite out of your wallet!

An Appendix Appendix

I was in the hospital for exploratory surgery," says the recovering patient, "and since they were inside me anyway, they went ahead and took out my appendix. After all, it's not good for anything and it can cause trouble, so why not get rid of it when you have the chance?"

The poor appendix gets no respect. Like the tonsils, no one thinks about it much until it has to come out. A ruptured appendix, spilling bacteria out of the intestines into the abdominal cavity, can be fatal, so it's natural to be wary of this mysterious little organ. However, it isn't completely useless.

We're talking about the *vermiform* (Latin for "worm-shaped") appendix. There are other appendices in the body, such as the one on the mesenteries (tissues that connect internal organs to the abdominal wall), but they rarely cause any trouble. Botanists also use the word *appendix* to describe elognated parts of leaves or flower petals.

The vermiform appendix isn't as important to us as its equivalent organ in some animals is to them. In the same position where humans, wombats, and mice have an appendix, rabbits and some other animals have an exceptionally large *cecum* (Latin for "blind"; the cecum is a sort of blind alley, or dead end, in the intestine). The rabbit's cecum acts like a compost heap, enabling the animal to digest the fiber that makes up so much of its diet. Humans, on the other hand, don't digest fiber; it goes straight through, as those appetizing essays on the backs of cereal boxes tell us.

But although the appendix doesn't help us extract nutrition from rabbit food, it does at least protect against infections in its little corner of the gut. The appendix is a mass of lymphatic tissue (as are the tonsils), where the immune system can collect and remove bacteria we swallow along with food. Unfortunately, the appendix's connection to the intestines is very narrow, so it's easy for material to get stuck in it, fester, and eventually cause it to rupture.

On balance, the appendix may be more dangerous than helpful. But it is not, as is commonly believed, a "mere vestigial organ."

Did Mohawks Wear Mohawks?

THE Mohawk haircut: a head shaved bare except for a two-inch-wide strip of hair standing erect from forehead to neck. Why is it called that?

To begin with, it isn't called that—not everywhere, anyway. The English call it a Mohican haircut, and they're more historically accurate than those who call it a Mohawk. Mohawks and Mohicans are two completely different peoples.

The Mohawk Indians were members of the Iroquois League who lived (and still live) in what is now Quebec and upstate New York. The real-life Hiawatha was a Mohawk and was one of the founders of the league, around 1570. Contrary to Longfellow's famous poem, he was not a Chippewa from "the shores of Gitche Gumee" (Lake Superior).

The Mohicans, or Mohegans (meaning either wolf or river people), on the other hand, lived in Connecticut and belonged to a loose association of about fifteen tribes along the Atlantic coast who spoke very similar languages of the Algonquian linguistic family. The tribes also shared similar customs. "The men went bare-headed, with their hair fantastically trimmed, each according to his own fancy," wrote John DeForest in his 1851 *History of the Indians of Connecticut*. "One warrior would have it shaved on one side and long on the other. Another might be seen with his scalp completely bare, except a strip two or three inches in width running from the forehead over to the nape of the neck. This was kept short, and was so thoroughly stiffened with paint and bear's grease as to stand up straight"—in other words, some Mohicans wore Mohawks.

The Mohawks, on the other hand, seemed to prefer the half-bald, half-long look, with the hair on the unshaven side tied in a knot with feathers attached, according to an English missionary who visited them in 1713. A statue of the Mohawk leader Thoyanoguen ("King Hendrick") in Lake George, New York, shows him with something resembling a Mohawk, but the whole front half of the statue's head is bald, so the haircut is at most a half-Mohawk. Many paintings of Mohawks show a third style: the head mostly bald, except for a single tuft of hair on top or in the back, adorned with feathers.

The words *Mohawk* and *Mohican* have had varied careers in the English language. Around 1710, a gang of aristocratic hooligans called the Mohicans terrorized the streets of London. The "inside forward Mohawk" has been the name of a figure-skating maneuver since the 1880s. And in the mid-nineteenth century in England, for reasons unknown, *Mohican* was a slang term for a fat man who rode long distances in a horse-drawn omnibus. Honest Injun, Kimosabe!

Gray Versus Grey

THE old *gray* mare, she ain't what she used to be. She used to be *grey*. But what's the difference?

During most of the twentieth century, the difference has been primarily geographical: gray is American, grey is British. A hundred years ago, however, an informal poll by the *Oxford English Dictionary*'s editor showed that for many people the two words described subtly different colors. An 1885 technical manual, *Field's Chromatography*, spelled it out in detail. *Grey* was a simple mixture of black and white, while *gray* was somewhat darker, with a hint of red or brown thrown in. But even back then, not everyone agreed. The *Times* of London had always used *gray* exclusively, while other reputable printers had always spelled it *grey*.

Some etymologists (people who study the origin of words) have tried to make a case for one spelling or the other by making analogies between modern words and their Old English equivalents. Words ending in "-ay" have predecessors with certain attributes in common, while the ancestors of words ending in "-ey" have other similarities. The *Oxford English Dictionary* says that the results of those investigations are ambiguous. Gray, it points out, *is* more phonetic—but when has English ever been a phonetically spelled language? In one of its rare ventures into prescription rather than description, the *OED* says that in spite of technical distinctions made in the past, we should make no distinction in meaning between the two spellings.

Mt. Rushmore: Just Another Face in the Cloud?

W<small>HAT</small> do George Washington, Thomas Jefferson, Abraham Lincoln, and Theodore Roosevelt have in common, aside from having been presidents of the United States? They are the four faces carved on Mt. Rushmore in South Dakota, of course. But why those four? Why not include James Madison, father of the Constitution? Or Andrew Jackson, champion of democracy (for white males, at least)? Or Hiram Ulysses Simpson (U.S.) Grant, victorious Union commander? Or McKinley or Wilson or any other president?

The idea of carving several presidents' likenesses on Mt. Rushmore was born in a conversation between the South Dakota state historian, Doane Robinson, and sculptor John Gutzon de la Mothe Borglum, in 1924. Soon thereafter, a lead tablet bearing the French coat of arms and the date 1743 was dug up by accident in South Dakota. It had been buried by Pierre de La Verendrye, an explorer who had traveled up the Missouri River as far as Wyoming in search of the Pacific Ocean. Its discovery gave Borglum and Robinson the idea that the theme of the Mt. Rushmore sculpture should be the Louisiana Purchase—the acquisition of a huge tract of French territory (including South Dakota) by the United States in 1803.

According to Borglum's widow, the sculptor slightly altered this theme and decided to create a work of art concerned with the nation's expansion across the American continent. George Washington qualifies because he, more than any other individual, was responsible for founding the independent republic. So does Thomas Jefferson, who was president when the Louisiana Purchase was made. Teddy Roosevelt's charge up San Juan Hill was a celebrated event in the Spanish-American War; as a result of that war, the U.S. acquired the Philippines and other territories. Moreover, Roosevelt had spent a lot of time in the badlands of Mt. Rushmore's home state and was something of a local hero.

What about Lincoln, then? A great president, of course, but how is he connected with South Dakota, territorial expansion, or the Louisiana Purchase (which occurred before he was even born)? The explanation remains unclear. Mrs. Borglum, in an essay published in 1941 by the government's Mt. Rushmore National Memorial Commission, said Lincoln was included because he was the "President under whom Alaska was acquired" and therefore fits in with the expansion-across-America theme. A nice trick if true, since Lincoln died in 1865 and we bought Alaska from the Russians in 1867. Mrs. Borglum also pointed out that Lincoln was the "saviour of the republic," so if he didn't have anything to do with the expansion of the Union, at least he kept it from shrinking.

Later government publications dropped the erroneous statement about Lincoln and told a completely different story. The National Park Service's current brochure on Mt. Rushmore, which is based in part on a book by the sculptor's son, Lincoln Borglum, says: "These four figures symbolize the birth and trials of the first 150 years of the United States. Individually they represent the ideals of the Nation. George Washington signifies the struggle for independence and the birth of the Republic, Thomas Jefferson the idea of representative government, Abraham Lincoln the permanent union of the States and equality for all citizens, and Theodore Roosevelt the twentieth-century role of the United States in world affairs." Many historians would challenge the suggestion that Lincoln believed in "equality for all," but even if this explanation contains some questionable historical interpretation, at least it doesn't contain any errors of fact. Borglum himself never gave specific reasons for his choice of the four presidents, so the explanations by his wife and son are the closest we have to his own thinking.

It took fourteen years for Borglum (and, after his death, his son) to carve the mountain into its current shape. Even after all that effort, the sculpture is still incomplete: some of the details on the sides of the heads, for example, were never finished. But money for the project ran out in 1941, and there are no plans for any further work on the monument.

Scab-Snorting and Other Vaccines

IF you still need a reason to be grateful you don't live in a remote area of Afghanistan or Ethiopia, think about this the next time you go to the doctor to get your "shots": Until just a few years ago, people in those parts of the world were immunized against smallpox by having dried, powdered scabs from victims of the disease blown up their noses. This treatment, the oldest known form of vaccination, was invented by a Chinese Buddhist nun in the eleventh century.

Smallpox was so common in England in the 1790s that few people had a complexion unblemished by the disease. Few, that is, except for dairy maids. Dr. Edward Jenner noticed this fact and speculated that the dairy maids were more likely than others to contract *cow*pox because of their work around cattle, and thereby developed an immunity to the more serious disease *small*pox. Jenner experimented by inoculating human subjects with cowpox, letting the disease run its course, then exposing them to smallpox. These tests proved his theory right, but widespread application of the discovery was slow in coming, because the vaccine was not easy to produce, store, or ship in quantity.

The modern era of vaccines that could be produced in the laboratory and given to large numbers of people began, like so many scientific discoveries, by accident. One day around 1880 Louis Pasteur, who had been away from his lab on a holiday, returned to find that he had mistakenly left a culture of chicken cholera exposed to the air. Although the bacteria were weakened, Pasteur went ahead and used them in his experiment, and found that they provided immunity for chickens against virulent cholera bacteria, without harming most of the chickens.

After developing vaccines for other diseases of livestock, Pasteur produced a rabies vaccine for humans in 1885. Some of the recipients died from the inoculation, and the medical community was bitterly divided over the value and ethics of human vaccination. In 1899, opponents of the use of typhoid vaccine managed to prevent the treatment of British soldiers, with the result that fifty-eight thousand men fighting in the Boer War in South Africa caught the disease and nine thousand died.

There was, and is, a danger of ill effects from vaccination, including coming down with the very disease you are trying to prevent. The ancient powdered-scabs-up-your-nose treatment often developed into smallpox, which the patient then passed on to others. Even vaccines made from attenuated (weakened) strains of a disease can cause adverse reactions. Just as rubella (German measles) can cause arthritis, the vaccine against this disease can cause a form of joint pain known as catcher's crouch in about one out of every four adults, but it isn't dangerous. Measles vaccine causes encephalitis in one out of a million cases, but rash and high fever are more common. Typhoid and yellow-fever vaccines can result in fever and headaches.

In any case, you're better off with the vaccine than with the disease. So go get inoculated—unless, that is, you live in a remote village in Afghanistan.

Dukes and Earls

THE guest list for your dinner party includes Lady Godiva, Count Basie, the Marquis of Queensberry, Earl Grey, the Red Baron, Lord Tennyson, and the Duke of Earl. Do you know who outranks whom or what to call them when they arrive?

If there were any *royalty* coming to your party (which there isn't—that guest list contains only members of the *nobility*), they—kings, queens, and royal princes and princesses—would of course come first. And in England, the two Anglican archbishops rank just below them. Then come duke and duchess; marquis and marchioness; earl (or count, a different word for the same thing) and countess; viscount and viscountess; and baron and baroness. In England, bishops weigh in just above barons.

To make sure you pronounce their titles correctly, remember that the *s* is silent in *viscount*, and *marchioness* is MAR-shon-ess, as if she were a woman from the red planet.

Dukes and duchesses are called "Your Grace"; barons and baronesses are "Lord and Lady So-and-so"; and the rest you can just call by their titles.

If this seems complicated, be happy you're not living in prerevolutionary Russia, where you'd have to call members of the nobility *vashe vysokoprevoskhodityelstvo*

("Your Exalted Excellency"). For that matter, be happy you're not the queen of England, who has to address her nobles in various intricate formulas like "our right trusty and right entirely beloved cousin."

Many of these noble lords hand their titles down to their eldest sons, but there are also many "life peers" in Britain, whose titles die with them. Life peerages have existed on and off for centuries, but their systematic use began in 1870 as a device for putting distinguished but non-noble judges into the House of Lords (which is Britain's supreme court). Since 1958, life peerages have been used to honor worthy citizens, male and female, from all walks of life, and there are now hundreds of life peers.

What the Peace Symbol Really Means

THE peace symbol of the 1960s is becoming popular again. Entrepreneurs use it to sell souvenirs to nostalgic baby boomers, teenagers use it as a fashion accessory, and ordinary citizens use it to make a political statement. But almost no one knows its origin or its many meanings.

A common story, not quite correct, is that it was invented by the mathematician and philosopher Lord Bertrand Russell in 1958 and that it consists of the semaphore signals for the letters N and D, for "nuclear disarmament," superimposed on each other. It's possible that this story was spread by a misunderstanding of Henry Dreyfuss's *Symbol Sourcebook*, which states that Russell "introduced" the peace sign. In fact, the symbol was first used at a peace march in England on Easter weekend 1958, sponsored by the Campaign for Nuclear disarmament (CND), whose president was Bertrand Russell. It would have been very cumbersome for those 1958 protestors to carry banners with the long phrase "Unilateral Nuclear Disarmament," so necessity became the mother of invention. Gerald Holtom, an artist and CND member, came up with the symbol, which the *Manchester Guardian* newspaper described as "a sort of formalized white butterfly."

The semaphore signals for N and D (arms held at 4 and 8 o'clock, and 12 and 6 o'clock, respectively) inside a circle, representing the whole world, do indeed make up the symbol. But Holtom and other artists in the CND have pointed out that the symbol had other meanings, too. Take the circle away and it looks like a stick figure of a person with arms outstretched—"the gesture of a human being in despair." That same figure also traditionally represents "the death of man." The circle around it stands for not only the world, but also a womb or unborn child. And the black background—the symbol was originally always white on black—is supposed to stand for eternity.

Advocating nuclear disarmament is not the same thing as pacifism, so calling the symbol "the peace sign" is not strictly correct. But calling it "the symbol of the Campaign for Nuclear Disarmament" is probably not going to catch on, so the shorter phrase is likely to stay with us.

Just $999.95!

Fifty-nine cents for a can of beans. Why don't they just call it sixty cents and make it a nice round number? Possibly because they sell a lot more cans at fifty-nine cents than at sixty, but no one has done much solid research on this. It's just something that all retailers seem to take on faith. One third of all retail food prices end in the digit 9.

Economists have theories about why so many prices end in that digit. The practice may have started when most food was sold fresh, by the pound, rather than packaged in fixed sizes. Odd numbers make it just that much harder for consumers to figure out the cost of a half- or quarter-pound in their heads, so more people wind up buying a whole pound. That may explain why prices *used* to end in odd digits, but why would the habit persist today? And why 9 more than any other digit?

Odd-numbered prices survived because (1) we have a free-market economy; and (2) we don't really have a free-market economy. Because of the free market and competition, everyone in an industry tends to settle on standard practices that are good for the industry and acceptable to the consumer. These standard practices may remain in place long after the original logic or market forces that motivated them have disappeared. Prices ending in 9 became traditional because, for whatever reason, businesses believed that they worked; then packagers and wholesalers began designing products and setting price policies by working backward from an assumption that the retail price would end in 9 (or 5, the next most popular digit). The large firms that dominate many industries have tended to stick with these practices, because the retail-store owner (who has to juggle many different prices in his head when deciding which product to buy at wholesale) looks unfavorably on the seller who deviates from the pricing or packaging standard that everyone in the industry is familiar with.

But why 9 or 5 more often than 1, 3, or 7? One theory is that consumers think of prices in multiples of 5 cents: 50, 55, 60, 65, 70. If an item costs 59 cents, the consumer thinks he's getting a 1 cent discount from the "real" price of 60 cents; but at 61 cents, he thinks the store is trying to charge him an "extra" penny. If a seller worries that consumers would reject a rise from 59 to 69, he may settle on 65, which is an odd number and a multiple of 5 (that is, a "fair" price in the consumer's multiple-of-5-obsessed mind).

One study, conducted by economist Lawrence Friedman of the M&M Candy Co., tracked a product that sold for 49 cents in about half of the retail stores, with most of the remaining stores charging a discounted price of 43 or 47 cents. (Note that the most common price ended in a 9; the others ended in odd numbers, with 5 being avoided presumably because it wouldn't look like a discount.) Then the wholesaler raised its price. To retain the same profit margin, a retail store originally charging 49 cents would have had to adjust the price to 53 cents for the item, and at first, many did. But soon 55 cents became the most common retail price: it's the closest number to 53 that ends in a 9 or a 5.

Multiple pricing ("2 for 69 cents") increases sales dramatically. One store marked its 33-cent cans of tomato sauce

"3 for 99" and sold 70 percent more, even though the price per can works out to be the same.

Do grocers think we consumers are stupid to fall for these tricks? Do they laugh at us behind our backs? Maybe so, but we can laugh right back at them. Even *wholesale* prices, which the grocers themselves pay, end in 9 more often than they end in a nice round zero.

Montezuma's *Real* Revenge

COLOMBIAN coffee. Irish potatoes. Szechuan hot peppers. Italian tomato sauce. Central American bananas. Virginia ham. Those places and foods would go together in any word-association test.

Every one of those foods, though, was completely unknown in the place we think of as its "traditional" home, until Columbus came to America. They were all part of the great biological exchange between the old world and the new.

Europeans brought cows, swine, sheep, goats, rice, wheat, coffee, and bananas to America; they took home potatoes, tomatoes, kidney and lima beans, peanuts, peppers of all sorts, and corn (which became a staple crop in China by 1600)—as well as an important item of medical technology, the enema tube.

Unfortunately, the old and new worlds exchanged diseases, too. Measles, which the Europeans considered no more than an annoyance, was deadly to the Americans, who had no immunity to it. On the other hand, European explorers contracted and brought home something new to them: syphilis. As one historian has remarked, "this, rather than diarrhea, was the true 'Montezuma's Revenge.' "

In Which We Go in Search of the @#$%&*! Who Invented the Business Suit

Men who don an uncomfortable necktie every morning before work may find it hard to believe, but the standard business suit really was a good idea once upon a time. Most historians of clothing credit (or blame) the French Revolution for the business suit. Until about 1700, many European countries had legally enforceable dress codes, called sumptuary laws, for different social classes. For example, in fifteenth-century England, only lords were allowed to wear purple (a color long associated with royalty and high status) or clothes made of sable fur; only knights could wear satin, ermine, or velvet; and no one but the upper classes could wear shoes extending more than two inches beyond the toes. (Some medieval fops wore shoes almost a *yard* long, drawing ridicule from popular entertainers.) As new middle classes arose and social mobility became possible, these laws became harder to enforce. The French Revolution was a final, dramatic episode in this trend and spread ideas of democratization and social leveling. In lieu of expensive, fancy costumes, more and more men began wearing a simple uniform that evolved into today's business suit.

Why men and not women? The ideal of equality is a political and economic one, and men were much more involved than women in the world of politics and business.

81

At least, so goes one theory—and it seems to be borne out by the fact that women, who are entering business and politics in greater numbers, are adopting a standard business suit of their own.

Psychiatrist J. C. Fluegel, author of *The Psychology of Clothes*, lists these advantages of having a universally accepted form of clothing: It decreases social competition; keeps people from wasting time deciding what to wear; enables people who have no taste in clothes to feel confident that they are wearing the socially correct outfit; saves money that would otherwise be spent buying each year's new style; and protects clothing industry workers' jobs from the economic perils of fashion whim.

Now, the bad news. As Fluegel notes, the uniform business suit suppresses people's expression of their individuality. And the particular kind of costume our society has chosen is not very adaptable to different climates: people in hot and humid cities like Houston, for example, bundle themselves up in sweltering business suits every day and then pay Texas-size electric bills for air-conditioning. Moreover, during the past hundred years, human pride, vanity, and competition have managed to divest the business suit of its original symbolism of social equality. The standard uniform was transformed back into a status symbol. By the late nineteenth century, if a gentleman wanted to be socially correct, he had to be able to afford several different suits for different occasions and times of day. The lowest common denominator of that era, the sack suit, was good at camouflaging the bodily imperfections of sedentary, potbellied, urban capitalists, but its proportions looked odd on a well-built, muscular worker, so it highlighted social class distinctions.

Nevertheless, it can be dangerous to wear something other than the uniform society demands, or even to unbutton your collar—and not just because you could lose your job. In 1979, the pilot of a 747 returned from the lavatory to the cockpit with his tie loosened and his collar open. The collar snagged a fire-emergency handle, which immediately shut down one of the engines. No one was hurt, but the pilot can now add another reason to Dr. Fluegel's list of advantages of the tight, stiff, uncomfortable but universal male business suit.

The Feather or the Fist: Braces and Beyond

"**I** CAN hit a tooth with my fist, even two thousand times a day, day after day, and I'll make it sore, but I can't move it. But if I lay a feather on the tooth and leave it there, I *can* move it."

That statement by orthodontist William Gurley sounds as farfetched as the boast of Archimedes, who, explaining the physics of the lever, said that if he had a place to stand, he could move the earth itself. But Dr. Gurley's statement is essentially correct. Light but constant pressure will reposition teeth in the gums; intermittent pressure, no matter how strong, will not (although it could *break* the teeth). Actually, the pressure needed is a little more than what a feather would exert, but as little as five ounces' worth will do the trick.

Dr. Gurley cites a sad case that illustrates the point. As a dental student in the 1960s, he helped treat a child who, a couple of years before, had accidentally put some lye into his mouth. The insides of his cheeks were scarified and exerted pressure on his teeth; and his tongue had been almost completely dissolved by the chemical, so there was no counteracting pressure from inside. By the time the child was brought to the dental clinic, the imbalance of pressure had made all his teeth point inward and backward at an incredible angle.

84

Would-be orthodontists have been trying for thousands of years to find ways of exerting that constant lightweight pressure on teeth. There is archaeological evidence that the ancient Egyptians and Incas tried their hands at it. The father of modern dentistry, Pierre Fauchard, wrote up twelve case histories of patients to whose teeth he had applied "bands," or braces, in 1728, but hardly anyone else tried the idea until a little over a century ago.

Modern orthodontics got its start with suggestions published by Dr. William Magill of Erie, Pennsylvania, in 1871, and first put into practice by Dr. Edward Angle, of Minneapolis and Chicago, seventeen years later. Angle's first orthodontic device was called the expansion arch. Dentists around the world made this and other orthodontic appliances in their own offices, with their own hands, using plans published by Angle and his colleagues. By 1901, entrepreneurs had gotten into the act, offering prefabricated braces for sale to dentists. Angle began patenting some of his designs, stirring up a big controversy in the fledgling orthodontic profession over the ethics of such business ventures.

Another bitter argument erupted at the 1911 convention of the American Association of Orthodontists. The debate, on the issue of tooth extraction in orthodontic treatment, was described in the association's official history as being "near violent." Angle's system ruled out extraction, but today it's a common practice in orthodontics.

By the 1950s, orthodontists had designed a plethora of devices for the mouth, some of which, one orthodontist has said, "looked like the Nazis designed them." For example, to cure "tongue thrust," which was thought to cause malocclusion (overbite), some orthodontists used sharp spikes that pointed inward and pricked the tongue when the patient swallowed. A less painful alternative involved a 9-volt battery hooked up to electrodes, giving the tongue a mild buzz when it pushed too far forward. Some dentists sent patients to hypnotists in the hope that autosuggestion would alter the tongue's motion. In recent years, however, research has shown that tongue thrust does not reposition teeth at all. The cause-and-effect relationship is actually the other way around; patients with malocclusions can't easily close their lips fully when swallowing, so the tongue moves forward to provide the necessary seal. Intermittent pressure exerted by the tongue, during swallowing, can't cause teeth to move; it may be *stronger* than a feather, but it's not *constant* enough.

Recently, dental researchers have discovered why constant pressure is so much more effective than intermittent force. When braces slightly distort the teeth, jaw, and other nearby bones, a small electric current is generated in the mouth. This effect, called piezo-electricity (piezo, pronounced pea-AY-zoh, is from the Greek word for "pressure"), occurs whenever pressure is applied to certain minerals, especially quartz crystals but also bones. The electricity, in turn, stimulates the production of osteoclasts (bone-dissolving cells), which loosen the teeth and allow them to move in response to the force of the braces.

Once the relationship between electricity and osteoclasts was discovered, orthodontists wondered whether they could speed up tooth movement by applying additional current to the mouth. In a 1980 experiment, researchers put braces on cats and inserted electrodes in some of the cats' mouths. The teeth of the cats who'd been hooked up to the local, mild (15 microampere) current moved twice as fast as those of the control group. Even an external electromagnetic field can enhance the work of braces. Experimenters in 1987 fitted some guinea pigs with braces and put half of the animals near coils of wire carrying 4.5 amperes at 15 volts pulsing on and off twenty-five times a second. Ten days later, the zapped guinea pigs' teeth had moved about 25 percent farther than the control group's. Orthodontists don't use these methods on human patients yet because there may be harmful side effects. Implanted electrodes can damage the nearby tissue; the guinea pigs in the 1987 experiment showed changes in their blood chemistry; and neither of the experiments investigated what happens after more than a few days of treatment.

Chemicals can also cause osteoclasts to form and thus speed up the movement of teeth. Hormone-like substances called prostaglandins will do the trick, but they cause inflammation. A less irritating substance, vitamin D, sped up tooth movement by 60 percent when injected into the gums of cats wearing braces.

Orthodontists can even prevent some problems before they occur. If a child loses a baby tooth (in an accident, for example) before the permanent tooth is ready to come in, a simple appliance can keep the adjacent teeth from moving together and blocking the open space. If X rays reveal that a permanent tooth is moving sideways and is threatening to become impacted, removal of the corresponding baby tooth and widening of the resulting socket can coax the wayward tooth into the proper channel. And if a child's maxillary arch (upper jaw) is growing faster than his mandible (lower jaw), he can be fitted with a face bow, which retards growth of the arch so that the mandible can catch up.

Space Rescue

W HEN the Apollo 13 astronauts first radioed, "Houston, we've got a problem," no one knew whether they would ever return to earth or be marooned in space.

Since then there has been a lot of research and a lot of talk about how to rescue helpless space travelers, but mostly it remains just that—talk. "Today, if you're stranded in space, you're stuck," says one space scientist. But with the prospect of more and more people going into space for industrial purposes as well as research, space agencies and aerospace manufacturers around the world are putting more effort into rescue technologies.

If large-scale, permanently manned space stations are ever built, rescue will become much easier than it would be today. Space stations would probably be located about six thousand miles above the earth, while most other manned space flights would be at altitudes below five hundred miles. Rescue missions from the space station could thus be launched *down*, not up, requiring less fuel, and there would be no problems with weather delaying the launch.

But there are no such large space stations now, and won't be for years. There are, however, already some devices and systems that could be useful in a space rescue. The NAVSTAR Global Positioning system, a network of satellites, can pinpoint an object in orbit to within a few yards. Space suits are designed with life-support systems to allow astronauts to move in a vacuum from one spacecraft to another. Astronauts who have to bail out can zip themselves into a Personnel Rescue Sphere, a womb-like shell that can keep a person alive temporarily while waiting for rescuers. A Manned Maneuvering Unit—a large backpack with twenty-four thrusters—can propel a rescuer to a victim so that he can hook onto the space suit or Rescue Sphere and transport the person to safety. There's even a robot under development, called the EVA (extra-vehicular activity) Retriever, that would eliminate the need for human rescuers to leave their spacecraft.

Other rescue ideas that have been proposed include:

• An ejectable capsule that can orbit, reenter the atmosphere, and survive at sea for twenty-four hours. (The French "Hermes" space plane will have one of these.)
• A pre-positioned rescue unit, manned or unmanned, waiting in orbit or stationed on the surface of the earth or moon.
• The "buddy system": crew and payload launched in separate, identical vehicles, each maneuverable by remote control and each usable as a rescue vehicle if the other becomes disabled.

Even if all these systems existed, a stranded spaceman could still be in trouble. An American astronaut going to rescue a Soviet cosmonaut may need to pump oxygen into the Soviet's space suit, but if the American oxygen hose and the Soviet intake valve aren't compatible, the cosmonaut might still asphyxiate. Scientists from both the U.S. and the U.S.S.R. have called for international standardization of such things, but so far, little has been done— less for reasons of national security than because of bureaucratic inertia.

One scientist's work on the standardization problem,

though, reportedly got him in trouble with his government. An American researcher sent a West German colleague the blueprints of the space suit hook that the EVA Retriever is supposed to be able to grab on to. NASA officials reprimanded him for revealing this "secret"—in spite of the fact that they had already sent the Germans some of the actual hooks, compliments of the U.S. government!

Will the Real Coca-Cola Please Stand Up?

APRIL 23, 1985: a date that will live in infamy. On that day, a beloved symbol of the American nation was desecrated. That was the day they introduced the new Coca-Cola.

Subsequently, we endured a silly spring and summer of press conferences, protest campaigns, advertising blitzes, disgusted consumers pouring new Coke into the gutter, and Peter Jennings interrupting *General Hospital* with the news flash that the abandoned formula would be reintroduced. Though it hasn't been very long since the event, there's already a whole mythology of mistaken popular beliefs about those ten weeks that shook the world.

Why was there such a big public outcry? Because it was the first time a popular soft drink had changed its formula? Hardly. Pepsi-Cola had changed its taste more than once in the past, in 1931 and again in 1983. At a 1959 trade fair in Moscow, Nikita Khrushchev said he could taste the difference between Soviet-bottled and American-bottled Pepsi. (Guess which one he liked better!) Coca-Cola had already changed, too. At the turn of the century, Coke (whose owner, Asa Chandler, was a teetotal abstainer from alcohol) contained cocaine. In those days customers would ask the soda jerk for "a dope" or "a shot in the arm." Although the substance was legal at the time, the company, eager to avoid controversy, dropped it from the formula in 1903 in the midst of a national agitation (which had racial overtones) for the outlawing of the drug. And in the 1980s both Coke and Pepsi authorized their bottling companies to use high-fructose corn sweetener instead of refined sugar. This negates the occasional argument that old and Classic Coke aren't the same because the former used only sugar and the latter, corn sweetener. In fact, old Coke had several different formulations (some of which contained corn sweetener) in the years before its replacement by new Coke.

In 1985, there were abundant disputes as to whether there really was a *perceptible* difference in the tastes of the old and new Coke products. These debates still arise, but they're more and more fruitless, since it's not easy to find a genuine old Coke for a taste test anymore. It *was* easy in 1985, though, and one taste test had embarrassing results: Seattle businessman Gay Mullins, one of the loudest agitators for the return of the old Coke, couldn't consistently identify the old and new in a series of blind taste tests. The authors, on the other hand, conducted their own blind test in 1987, using a precious antique can of old Coke, and identified the two samples correctly: the old Coke was less sweet and more fizzy than the new.

There are many theories regarding the Coca-Cola Company's decision to change its formula and tout the switch publicly, and about the ensuing outcry. Journalist Thomas Oliver has written about the Coca-Cola Company for years in the newspapers of Coke's hometown, Atlanta. He offers two explanations. First, in the early 1980s, Coca-Cola had just acquired a new generation of top managers, many of whom were foreign-born, including president Roberto Goizueta, a Cuban-American chemist, as well as executives hailing from Egypt, Mexico, and Argentina. These men, Oliver believes, didn't understand the deep sentimental attachment Americans have to Coke. Second, Oliver says, the Coca-Cola Company had diversified into enterprises (like Columbia Pictures) that had nothing to do with the soft-drink business and wasn't paying enough attention to its flagship product. When Coca-Cola executives finally noticed that Pepsi, which had kept its eye on *its* premier product, had been gaining market share, they panicked and changed their formula.

After the dust from the old Coke/new Coke wars had settled, some Pepsi executives advanced their own theory. They believed Coke. had simply overreacted to the "Pepsi Challenge," a mid-1970s ad campaign that featured average consumers choosing Pepsi over Coke in taste tests. The Pepsi Challenge *did* increase Pepsi's market share a bit, but at the expense of smaller colas, not Coke. (Pepsi's share went from 17.4 percent to 17.6 percent, while Coke's rose from 24.2 percent to 24.3 percent between 1975 and 1978.) Pepsi-Cola's analysts believe the Challenge hurt Coke's pride more than its pocketbook but nevertheless started Coke on the road to changing its formula. Pepsi's version of events has some support in the fact that Coca-Cola scientists *had* begun research into a new taste as early as 1979. The new Coke they eventually rolled out in 1985 was an obvious attempt to out-Pepsi Pepsi: The main change from old Coke was that the new product contained about one tenth more sugar, making it even sweeter than its challenging competitor.

New Coke will probably never have the mystique of the original drink, at least not if that mystique is based on public belief in a constant and unchanging formula. Just two months after the new Coke was introduced, it was being fiddled with again: New Coke was made less "flat," with higher doses of phosphoric acid and carbonation. In 1990, the company renamed new Coke to "Coke II" and test-marketed it (successfully, they said) in Spokane, Washington. You can hardly tell the players apart without a program. Can an Official Coca-Cola Vintage Chart be far behind?

C-C-C-A-A-A-R-R-R-T-T-T-O-O-O-O-O-O-N-N-N-S-S-S

SOMEBODY had to draw every frame of early animated cartoons by hand. How did they do such tedious work without losing their minds, or at least their comic imagination?

Only in the earliest years of the industry was a cartoon the product of one artist. The first cartoons may not look like much to us today, but audiences at the time were excited. Although jumpy movies of stick figures had been made before then, 1909 has been called the beginning of the era of animation. That was when *Gertie the Trained Dinosaur* was released. Cartoonist Winsor McCay drew all ten thousand frames that made up the film.

The first cartoons had no background at all; then came cartoons with the background drawn on each frame. During the silent-movie years of the teens and twenties, animators developed ways of making background drawing a little less tedious. The first step was phase animation: Draw a background and photograph the moving characters in front of it for several frames, then draw a slightly different background for the next few frames. By the 1920s, background drawing had become a specialized job, freeing the chief animator from the task altogether.

The first talking cartoons came out in 1928, including one from the Disney studios starring Mickey Mouse. Around the same time, Disney tried another new technique that took much longer to catch on than the talkies did: a film called *Alice in Cartoonland* mixed animation and live action. Richard Schickel, the unauthorized historian of Disney, said it was "quite crudely done." As late as 1971, film experts John Halas and Roger Manvell were saying that animation and live action "can merge no more easily than oil and water." But less than two decades later, *Who Framed Roger Rabbit* won an Oscar. Disney's experiment had taken sixty years to bear fruit.

Snow White and the Seven Dwarfs, the first full-length animated feature, was released in 1938. By that time, cartoon animation was big business, with many studios making short subjects to accompany feature films. At Disney, top animators' salaries were in the range of $150 to $200 a week—which was good money during the Depression. But at the same time, lower-ranking animators in the industry were making only one tenth of that. The cartoonists unionized.

The labor movement was comfortable with coal miners and steel workers but didn't know where to place these artists who drew talking mice. At first the cartoonists were put into the Brotherhood of Painters and Paperhangers—drawing and painting seemed related—but eventually they wound up in the International Alliance of Theatrical and Stage Employees. When they went on strike in the 1940s, though, once against Disney and once against Terrytoons, the animators didn't have much leverage. In both cases, the studios had a backlog of resources (either films or money) that enabled them to survive the strike longer than the workers could.

By the 1960s, animated cartoons had become so expensive to make that movie houses stopped showing them. Besides, the theaters and studios benefited more by subjecting their captive audiences to previews of coming attractions. A few movie animators held on, notably the creators of the Pink Panther. But more and more cartoons were being made for television instead.

New computer technology developed in the 1960s

helped animators do more work in less time. Some critics, however, complain that a lot of today's computer-generated animation is lousy because it is done by people with no experience in cartooning or art of any kind.

Despite automation, a lot of animation is done today the same way it's been done since the current division of labor in the industry was created in the 1920s. Characters are invented and a story is written. A key animator, the top cat of the cartoonists, draws some of the pictures for the cartoon—maybe one picture per second or half-second of actual running time—but in outline only, with no coloring-in and no backgrounds.

Inbetweeners, as their name implies, sketch the frames in between the ones drawn by the key animator. It takes twenty-four frames to make one second of running cartoon. The inbetweeners use very thin paper, so they can lay their pages on top of each other and still see the last four or five sketches. When cartooning for television, they don't need to take quite as much care with the characters' lip movements as when they're drawing for the big screen: TV audiences are less likely to notice if the mouths aren't quite in sync with the dialogue. Like the key animator, the inbetweeners draw only outlines of the characters.

When all the frames have been outlined, the artists do a line test—they see what the cartoon would look like if their skeletal drawings were made into a film—and make any necessary corrections. Then the background artist—often someone with a classical art education—draws the backgrounds for the cartoon.

The outlines of the foreground figures are copied onto transparencies, or cels (from *celluloid*), and then colors are added (on the back of the cels, so as not to obscure the black outlines on the front). The copying and coloring-in are often done by low-paid employees with little hope of advancement in the industry. Those tasks *can* also be done by the Xerox copier and the computer, respectively, but the results are less fuzzy if done by the human hand.

Even after all the drawing is finished, there is still plenty of work to be done. The drawings must be photographed. Sound tracks (voice, music, and sound effects) must be recorded. Then the pictures and the sound have to be synchronized with each other.

Before leaving the world of animation, there's one other question people often ask about cartoons: Why do so many characters have only four fingers on each hand? Mickey Mouse was one of the first four-fingered characters, and Walt Disney himself answered that question. The first reason was aesthetic: Mickey's hands were already large compared to the rest of his body, and putting five fingers on each one would have made them look grotesque. The other reason was one of simple efficiency (that's the scientific-sounding word for laziness): four fingers are 20 percent easier to animate than five.

Flying the Primitive Skies

THE first airlines were created for the purpose of carrying airmail. Passengers were just an afterthought, and in those early days, traveling by air was not always safe, easy, or pleasant.

Planes flying between London and Paris in 1919 carried no more than four passengers at a time in a closed but unheated cabin. There are often clouds over the English Channel, and the pilots flew *under* them, sometimes no more than forty feet above the water. Pilots carried enough British and French currency to buy railway tickets for all the passengers in case the plane broke down along the way; this happened so often the airline and railroads eventually agreed that their tickets would be interchangeable. At least it was easy to *find* a train if the aircraft had to make a forced landing: There were no navigational beacons, so pilots used railroad tracks as landmarks and flew right along them.

Horace Brock, a pilot who flew along the Caribbean coast of South America in the 1930s, wrote that his passengers often brought along "all their household pots and pans, chickens, children, and relatives." There were no toilets on the planes, so the passengers often used the seats instead. "Thank God," wrote the pilot, "natives cleaned the planes for us." (And the U.S. government still wonders why those "natives" don't always seem to like us?)

There were no aviation charts back then; pilots used sailors' navigation charts instead. One pilot looked for a big tree mentioned on a South American chart but didn't see any trees for miles around. Then he noticed a note on the chart explaining that it was "based on surveys by Magellan"—hundreds of years out of date.

Within a few years, by the late 1930s, a typical airline crew consisted of a pilot, copilot, steward, and Morse-code radio operator. Radio beacons made navigation somewhat easier and more precise than it had been, but even a simple rainstorm could put the transmitters out of commission.

Pan Am flew the first trans-Pacific flight in 1935, between San Francisco and Manila, but it wasn't nonstop. The China Clippers, as the unusual aircraft were called (there were only three of them), left San Francisco at 3 P.M. each Wednesday, arriving at Pearl Harbor eighteen hours later. From there, they went on to the islands of Midway and Guam, where there were Pan Am hotels in which passengers spent the night, arriving finally at Manila on Saturday. Each Clipper had a huge crew: two pilots, four copilots (doubling as backup engineers and radio operators), a navigator, a trainee, an engineer, a radio operator, and two stewards—all men. (Some airlines began hiring "hostesses" in the 1930s. The first ones were nurses, who wore their medical uniforms on the plane but did jobs like loading baggage and fueling the aircraft as well as serving drinks.) Passengers had upper and lower berths on either side of the fuselage, as if they were on a Pullman train. In the middle of the plane was a lounge with lightweight bamboo furniture for fourteen people. Forward of the lounge was the galley, and forward of that, the cockpit.

If an aircraft went down at sea, there was no hope of rescue. At least one China Clipper never arrived at Manila. No one ever found out what happened to it.

In spite of the dangers, though, some of those early flights were classier than today's utilitarian airplane trips.

The $50 fare between Los Angeles and San Francisco in 1928 covered not only air transportation but also a Cadillac ride to and from the airports. And everyone getting on flights from New York to Europe in the 1930s was given an elegantly printed list of all the passengers and crew, just as was done on ritzy ocean liners like the *Queen Mary*.

Neutral Zones

WHAT are those "neutral zones" that appear on maps of the Middle East? What countries do they belong to? And perhaps the first question that would come to mind about land in that part of the world: Who would profit if oil were discovered beneath them?

In 1922 a British diplomat, Sir Percy Cox, was serving as negotiator between King Ibn Saud of Nejd (now Saudi Arabia) and the ruler of Kuwait in their boundary dispute. Neither side seemed willing to compromise, and Sir Percy finally became so frustrated that he simply drew a straight line on a map to separate Nejd on the south from Kuwait and British-controlled Iraq on the north.

But before presenting his arbitrary boundary to the two monarchs, he realized that perhaps his line gave Iraq too good a deal and Kuwait a bad one. So he proposed that two plots of land be set aside as neutral zones—something never heard of before in international law—and that the countries bordering each zone split any future oil revenues half and half.

At the time, no one had found any oil in those areas, but geologists thought there might be some. In 1945, oil was discovered in the Kuwait/Saudi neutral zone, and twenty years later the two countries agreed to draw a regular boundary across the middle of the zone. But the two

101

countries continued to split the oil money from the area fifty-fifty. So although only the Iraq/Saudi zone appeared on maps, the Kuwait/Saudi zone also continued to exist for its most important purpose—money.

Iraqi dictator Saddam Hussein's invasion of Kuwait in August 1990 abruptly ended this arrangement. Condemning Sir Percy's boundary lines as western imperialist meddling, Saddam reasserted a decades-old Iraqi claim to ownership of Kuwait. Iraq occupied the whole country, even Kuwait's half of the Kuwait/Saudi neutral zone, which is supposed to be demilitarized. Ironically, Saddam had already profited for years from the neutral zone's oil: During most of the 1980s his two Arab neighbors had been donating all of their neutral-zone income to Iraq's war effort against Iran.

Castrati

"**W**ANTED: Boys, ages 6 to 8, with demonstrated musical ability, to be prepared for exciting and lucrative career. Meet famous composers and the crowned heads of Europe; save money on shaving cream. Apply University of Bologna, Medical School, Department of Genito-Urinary Surgery."

No such want ad ever appeared in seventeenth-century Italian newspapers, of course, but parents of talented boys knew the facts: They could have their son turned into a castrato and maybe, just maybe, propel him to wealth and fame in a singing career.

In Italy, as elsewhere, many people considered the theater to be a bad influence. Catholic Church officials in some cities tried to protect the morals of women by banning them from the stage. The unintended consequence was a demand for men with high voices to sing the female roles in operas. Even in times and places where women were permitted to appear onstage, some composers gave them only the alto parts, leaving the very lowest and very highest voices to men.

Castration was illegal, but it was well known that some doctors at Bologna's medical school performed it anyway. The operation was much less gory and disfiguring than might be imagined. The patient was sedated with opium or belladonna and soaked in a hot bath. No part of the body was actually removed; the testicles were left inside the scrotum but were disconnected from all blood vessels, glandular ducts, and other attachments to the rest of the body.

One result, obviously, was that the boy's voice never "changed"—that is, it never got lower in pitch or frequency. The *tone* of the castrato's voice *did* change as he grew up, however—for the better, we're told—because although he sang the same high notes a child would sing, the grown castrato had the lung power of an adult.

Castrati tended to be chubbier than other men, and taller. They could have sexual relations to some extent; some even married, although the Church officially prohibited it. At least one, Loreto Vittori (1600–1670), became a priest.

Their operatic heydey was from about 1600 to 1750, although Mozart wrote a few roles for them in the late eighteenth century, and Rossini used one as late as 1824. Castrati were expected to sing stunningly complex ornamentation, and composers often turned to them for advice when writing operas. At least one castrato gave advice in a more powerful realm: Carlo Broschi (1705–1782) was a confidant of the king of Spain and was unofficially, but de facto, the prime minister of that country for some years.

Castrati sang in church choirs long after they stopped appearing on the operatic stage. The Church barred them from joining choirs after 1861, but those who were already singing at that time were allowed to continue. The last castrato singer, Alessandro Moreschi, died in 1922. His musical career just barely overlapped the era of the phonograph: Moreschi can be heard on a 1903 recording of the Sistine Chapel choir.

The Italian practice of castration of young boys was relatively benign compared to the equivalent Chinese operation. To produce a eunuch, the Chinese cut off all the external genitalia, inserted a metal plug into the urethra (the tube leading out from the bladder), compressed the wound with bandages, and did not allow the patient to drink or urinate for three days. The wound took three months to heal.

At least Chinese eunuchs, unlike Italian castrati, were old enough to know what they were doing when they volunteered for that status. The operation may not have been pleasant, but it *was* a way to gain political power. Since the days of the Han dynasty (around 200 B.C.), Chinese royalty had allowed eunuchs to have free run of the palace and exercise political influence, because a eunuch could not have children and thereby start a rival dynasty. The last known Chinese eunuch underwent the surgery in 1929.

In the Scandinavian countries today, castration is available for use in the prevention of sex crimes. No one, not even a convicted rapist, is forcibly emasculated, but a criminal may be castrated if he requests the operation and if medical and legal officials determine that it would help him avoid future offenses.

Circle the Wagons!

They really did circle the wagons. It's not just a cliché from Hollywood westerns. Wagon trains traveling across the Old West circled the wagons, not only in emergencies, but routinely.

The wagon train was invented in 1832 by Captain Benjamin Bonneville, on leave from the army and doing business as a fur trader. He had been transporting his goods on pack animals but thought wagons would be more efficient: He wouldn't have to unload them at night, and it would take fewer horses and mules to pull wagons than to carry loads on their backs. Besides, he reasoned, he could use the wagons as a defensive shield against enemies.

Within ten years, Bonneville's idea had caught on among fur traders and others hauling goods out west, but at first there weren't many people engaged in those businesses. The Mormon settlement of Utah in 1847, though, created a large market for eastern goods in the West and began the heyday of the wagon train.

The popular image of a wagon train is a group of pioneer families moving west, but most wagon trains carried freight rather than emigrants. There are no exact figures—there was no central registry of wagon trains—but according to one estimate, over three quarters of all wagon trains carried merchandise, with only enough people and animals to get the goods safely to market.

Sometimes the animals were horses, but mules were better, because they could thrive on a diet of all grass and no grain. (Grass could be found along the way, but grain for horses had to be carried, and added to the weight of the wagons.) Oxen were even better: They shared the mules' food requirements but were less attractive to thieves. Besides, if food ran short, any animal could be eaten, but most settlers and wagon masters preferred beefsteak to mule stew.

But no matter which animals were doing the pulling, and regardless of the number of settlers along for the ride, they really did circle the wagons. They usually did it twice a day, once when they rested in the midday heat and again when they stopped for the night.

They didn't call it "circling" the wagons, though. They called it "corraling"—because they did it mainly to keep their animals in, rather than to keep attackers out. A typical train of about forty wagons would make an oval-shaped corral fifty by thirty yards in size. Competent drivers could set one up in about five minutes.

Indian attacks on wagon trains were not frequent except for a few years in the mid-1860s. As long as the wagons traveled through uncontested lands, they were usually safe. Freighters rumbling from Ft. Laramie, Wyoming, to Helena, Montana, preferred to take a four hundred-mile detour through Salt Lake City rather than use the Bozeman Trail. The Bozeman was more direct but passed through territory claimed and defended by Indians, who managed to close down the trail completely in 1863.

The next year, in misguided retaliation, Col. John Chivington and his Colorado Volunteers murdered hundreds of Indian men, women, and children in the Sand Creek Massacre. This provoked widespread Indian attacks on wagon trains all across the Great Plains. The government then forbade wagon trains to travel without a military escort. But extra troops were hard to find, since the army was busy finishing the Civil War and occupying the South, so wagon trains often had to wait. The result was traffic jams up to three miles long.

In 1865, a wagon train's herder found some arrows on the ground and, as a joke, stuck them through his hat and rode into Fort Halleck, Wyoming. Some of the soldiers who went out looking for the "attackers" got frostbite. The practical joker and his wagon master were arrested, and the resulting delay bankrupted the owner of the wagon train.

The transcontinental railroad, finished in 1867, was the beginning of the end for wagon trains. The wagons continued to roll for several years but eventually became a thing of the past and the stuff of myths, legends, and movies. Once upon a time, though, they really did circle the wagons.

How They Shell All Those Popcorn Shrimp

SEAFOOD restaurants sometimes offer a plate of a hundred or more very small "popcorn" shrimp, all shelled and fried. Boiled, shelled, tiny shrimp are available in cans and are served on salad bars and smorgasbords. Does someone have to peel all those shrimp by hand?

You *can* get hand-shelled, fancy-pack shrimp, but they are very expensive. Most shrimp processed in industrialized nations are shelled and deveined by machine.

First the shrimp's head is cut off (this is still sometimes done by hand). Then a machine positions the shrimp so that a knife can cut the shell down the back and expose the "vein," which is actually the shrimp's digestive tract. Next, the shrimp moves onto a bed of cylinders spaced closely together and rolling in opposite directions. These pinch the tail and pull the shell off but are too close together to let the shrimp meat fall between them. Instead, the meat slides down along the rollers (which are tilted, not level) and goes on to the deveining process.

The vein, exposed by the knife cut, is sometimes removed by tumbling the shrimp inside a cylindrical tank with a rough inside surface on which the vein snags. Alternatively, another machine positions the shrimp so that a small jet of water washes the vein out.

The main product of these operations, is, of course, the

shrimp meat, but the shells are useful too. They contain a substance called chitin, which is useful in waste-water treatment, paper manufacturing, food processing (as a thickener), and as a wound-healing agent. The shells can also be processed into a protein concentrate for animals or fed to salmon to make their flesh redder.

I've Been Working Like a Dog

THE ideal employee has rare and highly developed skills but is willing to work for peanuts. Businesses have often gone to foreign countries in search of the perfect worker, but they also frequently go to the animal kingdom instead.

Long before people invented the steam engine or internal combustion, our ancestors used quadrupeds to draw plows and carry burdens. Even in the high-tech United States, workhorses still plow some fields, and llamas still pack supplies to the hikers' lodge atop Mt. Leconte in Tennessee.

Animals have also been used for entertainment, and have often been treated badly in the process. One French lion tamer was so cruel that even Joseph Goebbels, the Nazi propagandist who later murdered his own children, complained about him. People flock to bullfights (legal in many countries) and cockfights (even though they are widely banned). Rodeos draw more and more criticism for practices like the use of tight straps and anal prodding to make broncos buck. Show horses are sometimes quietened down by bloodletting, nostril taping (to reduce oxygen consumption), and severing of their tail muscles (because motionless tails are an asset in some kinds of competitions). They may be made more animated by the administration of cocaine, by the application of ginger to the anus, or by exposure to electric current in a tub of water.

Bear baiting (in which a bear was confined on a leash while bulldogs, specially bred for this "sport," terrorized and tortured it) may be out of fashion, but the training of dancing bears is sometimes just as cruel. The animal, for example, may be forced to walk across a hot surface to teach it to raise its feet higher.

Movies and TV shows have often had animal stars, and although Hollywood signed an agreement in 1940 to cooperate (to some extent) with the American Humane Association, complaints continue. *The Day of the Locust*, for example, displayed a cockfight, and some animal-rights activists claimed birds were poisoned by hair spray used on them in *Jonathan Livingston Seagull*.

Animals have often been drafted into one of humankind's favorite activities, war. Hannibal's army used elephants (as well as horses) to cross the Alps in 218 B.C. During the Vietnam War, the U.S. military trained dogs to warn soldiers about land mines, trip wires, and punji pits (booby traps filled with sharp spikes). The dogs' keen noses could sniff out recently dug earth, explosives, and even the odor of unfamiliar people who had been in the vicinity. Dogs were also trained to stalk the enemy: not just to follow him, but to remain unseen.

The navy has not been lax in training animals for undersea warfare. Dolphins can use their sonar to distinguish thicknesses and compositions of metal plate, so as to tell "our" ships from "theirs" while the ships themselves maintain radio and sonar silence. They can locate different types of undersea mines. And they can communicate their findings to their human commanders.

These same skills can also be put to more constructive uses. Dogs can sniff out survivors in the rubble of a disaster, not just explosives in a mine field. Dolphins can use their metal-detecting hearing to locate sunken ships, airplanes that crashed at sea, and oceanographic instruments—a real bonanza, because merely searching for a lost item at sea can account for 90 percent of the cost of its recovery and salvage. Sea lions can not only find sunken objects but also attach cables to them.

John Lilly, an expert in animal/human communication, has speculated on the future of interactions between us and other creatures. He has made these suggestions, ranging from the mundane to the far out:

• Learning more about animals' languages may generate spin-off technologies, such as better computerized translation between human languages.

• If we could talk to the animals, we could ask dolphins or whales to locate tuna for fishing boats; then the fishermen could warn seagoing mammals away from the area before casting their nets.

• Dolphins could help prevent oil spills by warning of small underwater leaks, which they can smell. They could also help find new oil fields by carrying instruments during geological surveys of the ocean floor.

• Better communication could even improve entertainment for both humans and animals. Movie directors could give precise instructions to animal actors. Dolphins and whales could sing for humans, humans could play instruments or synthesize music pleasing to undersea creatures, or the two species could exchange ideas and make music together.

One thing these visionary futurists like Dr. Lilly probably haven't considered: If animal workers learn to communicate, how long will it be before they invent the labor union and the strike?

Jolly Rogers

A ROLLICKING band of pirates are we, with a yo-ho-ho, and a Jolly Roger, and a walk-the-plank, and a workers' compensation insurance plan"—a sea chantey that probably never was sung but could have been.

Workers' comp was a matter of course among pirates as early as 1700. The captain would pay a sailor for the loss of an arm or the loss of an eye, all guaranteed in writing. The payments, translated into modern currency, were about the same as they are for industrial workers today. Pirate work generated so many injuries that the Hollywood and comic-book image of the pirate with a peg leg or an eye patch is not at all inaccurate.

Now, about that "rollicking band" business. Most pirates did drink—brandy when they could get it, rum or wine at other times. After looting a ship, crews would often hide out on deserted islands, get drunk, and entertain themselves by staging mock trials at which they would boast of their exploits. (On one occasion, the gallows humor went too far: A crewman was "found guilty" and then executed by his reveling mates.) However, one captain, Bartholomew Roberts, ran a taut, but definitely not tight, ship. Roberts, who was active off New England around 1720, forbade drinking and gambling and strictly enforced lights-out at 8 P.M. every night. It may not have been much fun sailing with Roberts, but it was lucrative:

He holds the record for the number of ships plundered, about four hundred.

The Jolly Roger flag is another token of the pirate legend that actually existed, although it wasn't universal. No pirate flags of any kind have survived to the present day, but there are plenty of contemporary records describing flags that depicted skeletons (often holding a wineglass and a sword). At least one pirate, James Plantain, flew the classic skull and crossbones. Others simply displayed solid red or black flags.

Walking the plank, on the other hand, was not typical pirate entertainment. Historian Rayner Thrower writes that he knows of only one report of a sailor being made to walk the plank: on the ship of Derdrake, a Danish pirate, around 1700. When pirates took over a ship, they usually gave the captive sailors the choice of joining up with the crew or being tossed overboard (summarily, without the plank ceremony). In general, when pirates killed people, they did it with dispatch and without gratuitous cruelty. They tortured captives to find out where the loot was hidden but rarely did so for the sheer sadistic pleasure of it. There were a few exceptions: a French pirate, Mountbars the Exterminator, for example, once slit open a captive's belly, pulled out a short piece of intestine, fastened it to a tree, then chased the victim around with a flaming torch.

Women don't usually figure in the popular image of pirate crews. There were, however, several celebrated female pirates in Europe, America, and the Far East.

In the sixteenth century, Lady Killigrew of Falmouth, England, was able to ply her trade without interference from lawmen for many years, because her husband was the vice-admiral of Cornwall and her son was in charge of the local commission that was supposed to investigate incidents of piracy. Eventually, though, central-government authorities in London caught up with her and she was imprisoned.

Anne Bonney, an Irish immigrant to America, sailed

with her lover, "Calico Jack" Rackam, in the Caribbean in the early 1700s. When the British navy attacked them off Jamaica, only Bonney and her partner Mary Read stayed on deck to fight; all the men hid below.

In the early 1800s, Cheng I Sao, widow of the Chinese pirate Cheng I, carried on her late husband's business. She commanded three hundred ships and tens of thousands of men, and she *did* treat it as a business, keeping meticulous records that included bureaucratic doublespeak (such as "transshipped goods" for stolen loot). Cheng I Sao enforced strict discipline among her crews: Sailors found guilty of raping a female captive or withholding loot from the general fund were executed, and those who went AWOL were tracked down and had their ears cut off.

Another Chinese woman, Madame Hon Cho Lo, sailed as a pirate around 1920, but generally piracy was moribund during the late nineteenth and early twentieth centuries. As recently as 1952, a book on yachting discouraged the carrying of weapons on board, since there was no threat of thievery on the high seas. In recent years, though, piracy has returned with a vengeance. About fifty cargo ships disappear every year, and many more vessels, large and small, are robbed. Modern-day pirates prey on Vietnamese "boat people," and the victims get no protection from the navies of countries like Thailand, who don't want the refugees coming to their shores anyway. Pirates hijack yachts in the Caribbean, plunder cargo ships off West Africa, steal vessels from the shipping lanes between Greece and the Middle East, and even sneak aboard ships anchored in Singapore harbor and Manila Bay.

Robbery isn't the only crime committed on the oceans. In 1983, Massachusetts lawmen arrested the crew of a lobster boat, the *Honi-dew*, for possessing two deer without a hunting license.

Official State Symbols

THE tug-of-war at the Nelson County Fair has something that no other tug-of-war in the Commonwealth of Kentucky has. By act of the state legislature, it is Kentucky's one and only *official* tug-of-war.

Any state can have a boring old official state bird or state tree. But it takes imagination to have an official tug-of-war, air fair, American folk art symbol, beautification and conservation plant, or neckwear.

Before getting to those exotica, though, let's look at the most common state symbol of all—the state's name. Four states don't call themselves states at all: Massachusetts, Pennsylvania, Virginia, and Kentucky are commonwealths. But the U.S. Constitution doesn't recognize the distinction—to Uncle Sam, all fifty states are states, plain and simple. The longest state name belongs to the smallest state: "the State of Rhode Island and Providence Plantations."

Every state has a flag. In fact, some have more than one. Maine and Massachusetts have maritime flags in addition to their regular state flags, and several states have special flags for their governors. Kansas has a state banner, blue with a sunflower in the middle, which is different from the state flag. Oregon has only one flag, but its two sides are different: the front has the state seal, the back has a beaver.

Only eight states have pledges of allegiance to their flags; New Mexico has an official version in Spanish as well as in English. Probably the dumbest is Michigan's, which tries to be a rhyming poem but doesn't quite make it: "I pledge allegiance to the flag of Michigan and to the state for which it stands, two beautiful peninsulas united by a bridge of steel, where equal opportunity and justice to all is our ideal."

Almost every state has a state song. Maryland and Iowa use the same tune ("O Tannenbaum") but very different words, dating from the Civil War. "Maryland, My Maryland" has pro-Confederate lyrics even though the state didn't secede from the Union; Iowa's state song, written by a Northern soldier who had been held in a confederate prison camp, is an anti-Southern, antislavery reply to the Maryland song.

Some state songs are hardly known outside their own states, but others are popular tunes, like "You Are My Sunshine" (Louisiana), "Home on the Range" (Kansas), "Yankee Doodle" (Connecticut), and "On the Banks of the Wabash, Far Away" (Indiana). New Jersey, however, declined in 1980 to adopt Bruce Springsteen's "Born to Run."

In 1986 Kentucky changed the official lyrics of one line of its state song, "My Old Kentucky Home," from " 'Tis summer, the *darkies* are gay," to " 'Tis summer, the *people* are gay." But Virginia has never amended the 1940 law designating its state song, which contains these lines:

"Carry me back to old Virginia,
There's where the old darkey's heart am long'd to go.
That's where I labored so hard for old Massa . . ."

But on to the really important official state symbols:

ARIZONA	Neckwear	Bola tie
FLORIDA	Air fair	Central Florida Air Fair

	Litter control symbol	Glenn Glitter
KENTUCKY	Shakespeare festival	Shakespeare in Central Park (Louisville)
MARYLAND	Sport	Jousting
NORTH DAKOTA	Art gallery	UND Art Gallery, Grand Forks
OREGON	Hostess	Miss Oregon
PENNSYLVANIA	Beautification and conservation plant	Penngrift crownvetch
RHODE ISLAND	American folk art symbol	Charles I. D. Looff carousel
TENNESSEE	Fine art	Porcelain painting

Is Possession Nine Tenths of the Law?

REMEMBER back in elementary school, when you lost your lunch money or your favorite comic book? It was bound to be "found" (because it had been stolen in the first place) by some obnoxious kid who would refuse to give it back, chanting, "Finders keepers, losers weepers!" Or if he was really precocious, he might taunt you by yammering, "Possession is nine tenths of the law."

Maybe you were suspicious that the kid's legal reasoning wasn't on a par with that of Oliver Wendell Holmes. Well, both of you were partly right and both were partly wrong. True, an English court ruling of 1774 stated that "possession is very strong; rather more than nine *points* of the law." But the "possession" in dispute (a town's ownership of a toll road) had lasted for 350 years, and even so, the court said that "it is not very conclusive evidence."

The judge in that case didn't fabricate the phrase "nine points of the law." The saying had been around long before 1774. Originally, it was *"eleven* points of the law," an apparent reference to the twelve "points" of the compass. Whether twelve points, nine points, or nine tenths, the phrase suggests that possession is by far the most important kind of evidence in any lawsuit over ownership of property.

120

Under some circumstances, this is true. A person *possessing* a property can sue anyone but the rightful owner for the taking of, or damage to, the property, and recover just as much compensation as if he were the owner. In one of the few court cases on this point, in 1848, a Kentucky man who had taken in two stray horses successfully recovered $50 from a neighbor who shot the beasts for no good reason. The court ruled that the plaintiff did not have to prove ownership of the animals, just possession.

Even if the real owner *appears and proves his title,* a possessor still has some rights against a third party who steals or damages the property. The true owner recovers the property, but both he *and the possessor* can recover monetary damages from the third party.

It turns out, then, that possession is more tenths of the law than one might suspect. However, the rights of a possessor who isn't the legal owner may carry more weight on paper than in a courtroom. There is only one American case in which a person who possessed property against the will of the owner has recovered damages for trespass—and that was in 1830. Juries are apt to be less than sympathetic to the claim of a truly hostile possessor. In such a case, nine tenths of the law could turn out to be nine tenths of nothing.

Taco Bell's Got Your Order—Where the Hell Is the Border?

AFTER World War II, the story goes, a Russian officer knocked on the door of a farmhouse and introduced himself. "I am commander of border-surveying team," he said. "We will be drawing new Soviet-Ruritanian border nearby." "Well," the farmer asked, "what country will I be in?" "Before war, you were in Ruritania," replied the officer, "but now you are in glorious homeland of socialism, U.S.S.R." "Thank God!" said the farmer. "I don't think I could have survived another one of those cold Ruritanian winters!"

The new border probably didn't do that farmer any good, but a border is more than just an imaginary line on a map. In fact, borders are very real, and have real effects on individuals and whole economies. Just ask anyone who was jailed for trying to escape through the Iron Curtain—or ask the happy owner of a liquor store located on the "wet" side of an American county line.

Establishing a border today isn't done haphazardly or ad hoc; it's a well-defined process, and there are even textbooks spelling out all the procedural details.

First, let's get our terms straight. The actual line dividing two countries is the *boundary*. The *border* is a narrow band of territory on either side of the line. A *frontier* is a region, often unpopulated, where one country's jurisdiction gives way to another without a precise line between them.

There are boundaries at sea, on land, and in the air, each with its own peculiarities. The well-known three-mile limit on a nation's sovereignty over coastal waters got its start in the days when this was the range of most coastal cannons. The limit was just a statement of fact: A country could control the water over which it had firepower; beyond that, anyone was free to come and go. The three-mile limit is still recognized, but now it has a highly technical definition. A nation's maritime boundary is a line three miles from a low-water mark defined as the average of the two low tides "during the periods of 24 hours throughout the year when the maximum declination of the moon is 23 degrees 30 minutes." Nowadays, many countries claim more than three miles of ocean as their own.

There can also be *multiple* boundaries, associated with different privileges, between two nations. For example, one country may own mining and shellfish-gathering rights to a zone of water, while another owns the finfishing rights there. When the Antarctic Treaty expires in 1991, several long-dormant maritime boundary disputes are likely to boil over again, particularly concerning the waters surrounding the Antarctic Peninsula, which is claimed by Argentina, Britain, and Chile.

Even land boundaries are not always uniform. Belgium and the Netherlands, for example, have an underground boundary that differs from the surface boundary shown on maps. In 1950 they agreed to move the underground boundary so as not to divide coal mines between the two countries, thus increasing the efficiency and profitability of both countries' mines.

The *upper* limit of a country's jurisdiction has yet to be defined. There are several proposals on the table, most of them relying on some definition of *outer space*, which is an international realm. One suggestion is to define outer space as beginning—and a country's sovereign airspace as ending—at the altitude where aerodynamic flight becomes impossible (about sixty miles).

There aren't many new boundaries being drawn these days, but the process of constructing one is still important because it gives countries a standardized, peaceful way of resolving border disputes. There are three main phases: allocation, delimitation, and demarcation. *Allocation* is the most general and least technical of the phases. For example, country A lets country B have part of a valuable oil field in return for getting a region of country B where the people are ethnically related to country A—that sort of thing. *Delimitation*, the next stage, is an agreement on where the actual line will run. It's detailed but usually not precise or final. In most cases, the countries appoint a boundary commission with the power to move the line this way or that, within a certain tolerance or under certain conditions. Up to this point, the negotiations usually take place in some government office building far from the border itself. But in the final phase, *demarcation*, the boundary commissioners and their staff (surveyors, translators, laborers, drivers, local guides, etc.) go out in the field, make the final adjustments to the boundary, and erect markers along the line.

At the 1885 Berlin Conference, the European colonial powers (Britain, France, Germany, and others) allocated boundaries for their African colonies that were often arbitrary and were refined as exploration and boundary delimitation progressed. Many historians blame these arbitrary boundaries for disrupting whole peoples (like the Tuareg, whose homeland is now divided among the countries of Algeria, Libya, Mali, and Niger) and for the ethnic rivalries within some African nations today (notably Uganda). But in some cases, the colonial powers took care to redraw boundaries in order to keep small social units intact.

The legacy of the feudal system saved Europe from many of the problems Europeans imposed on other parts of the world with arbitrary, straight-line border allocations. For hundreds of years, Europe was divided into small fiefs and principalities along lines that more or less made ethnic and geographic sense.

The delimitation or description of the boundary can cause problems for boundary commissioners if it isn't carefully written. The Soviet-Latvian treaty of 1920 defines one point on the boundary as the place where a particular letter in a particular town name appears on the map but doesn't specify which map it's referring to. An Argentine-Chilean treaty of the 1880s placed part of the line along the division between two watersheds at the crest of a mountain range. When the surveyors arrived, they found that because of peculiar erosion patterns, the division between the watersheds followed a course that deviated from the crest of the mountains, so they didn't know which landmark to use. The boundary between Zaire and Sudan is also defined in terms of watersheds, but the land there is relatively flat, so it's difficult to determine the correct line. To this day, much of that boundary remains unmarked.

The curious zigzag in the North Carolina-South Carolina state line, just south of Charlotte, is a case in which boundary commissioners altered the line in consideration of local conditions. The commissioners drew the line that way in 1772 to avoid splitting the Catawba Indians between the two British colonies.

When final adjustments and surveys have been made, the boundary commissioners make the line visible. Much of the U.S.-Canadian border, for example, is a cleared strip twenty feet wide. And in 1960, the Chinese-Burmese border was marked by brightly colored flowering trees that don't usually grow in that area. The typical boundary marker, though, is a monument of stone or other permanent material. People living on the border, however, may destroy or shift the marker for various reasons. For example, if the monument is made of stone in an area where stone is scarce, someone may steal it to use for building materials. To help reestablish a boundary's location after one of these events, boundary commissioners sometimes bury a secret object, called a tell-tale, under each monument—something as fancy as a plaque or as simple as a broken bottle. In some cases, routine human activities help *preserve* the marking of the boundary. For example, the boundary commissioners for Ethiopia and British Somaliland cleared a footpath along the line; the scarcity of roads in that region made it likely that people would often walk the path, preventing its disappearance.

Long ago, some European societies took a very dim view of people who moved boundary stones. One ancient law provided that anyone who disturbed such a marker would be buried up to his neck in a field and have his head plowed off. The Romans executed farmers who disturbed boundary stones even accidentally and sacrificed the guilty party's oxen to Jove.

Occasionally boundary commissioners err, and another commission has to come back and move the markers to the true boundary. This has caused problems in several towns that grew up near the incorrectly marked U.S.-Canadian boundary, later to find that the real dividing line passes right through them. As it turns out, a few stores straddle the boundary—a customs nightmare for shoppers and merchants. However, one tavern owner has made the best of the situation: He put his pool table in the United States, where it's immune from a Canadian tax on billiards.

Tvyordy Znak

Aₓₜₑᵣ the communists took over Russia in 1917, they censored a lot of books, as the czars had before them, but they shortened Tolstoy's *War and Peace* by thirty-one pages without removing a single word.

Before the revolution, every word in the Russian language that ended in a consonant sound was spelled with one of the two letters ь or ъ at the end. The first of these letters, the *myakhky znak*, or "soft sign," changes the sound of the final consonant, but the other one, the *tvyordy znak*, or "hard sign," doesn't, and isn't really necessary.

The Soviet of People's Commissars decreed in 1918 that the *tvyordy znak* was no longer required at the end of a word (although there are some other situations where it is still necessary). The main reason for this and other spelling reforms was to make it easier for Russia's largely illiterate population to learn to read and write. But one of the beneficial by-products of eliminating this frequently used but useless letter was to reduce significantly the amount of paper needed to print books.

The Parthenon, the Eiffel Tower, and the Great Wall of China

THE Great Wall of China, the Parthenon, and the Eiffel Tower are among the most famous structures in the world. Yet most people haven't the foggiest idea why they were built in the first place.

The Great Wall? Doesn't everybody know that it was built to protect China against invasion? That's what the rulers who built the Great Wall (and other walls) claimed, but "there was no really desperate Frontier menace to be faced," according to historian Owen Lattimore. "The true purpose of both wall building and road building [in the third century B.C.] had to do with stabilizing the conquests that had been made in China itself, and with setting to rights a new order of society."

Several small feudal kingdoms in China began building walls around 300 B.C. Feudalism had reached its mature phase; rulers had conquered about all the new territory they could, so they wanted to make their borders permanent.

Over the next eighty years, the Qin empire gradually conquered the smaller feudal kingdoms, but after its final victory, it had a huge standing army with nothing to do. Seeing the danger inherent in an idle band of armed men, the government employed the soldiers in building roads and walls, including the Great Wall. As Lattimore points out, these were less for the public good than for the political strengthening of the empire.

On its western frontier, China gave way to the Central Asian steppes, and agriculture gave way to a nomadic economy. The Chinese could not occupy this area without becoming less involved in agriculture. Such a cultural change would have made China less homogeneous and possibly more decentralized, weakening the government's control. The Great Wall kept China's size manageable by limiting westward migration, thereby making it easier to rule centrally.

(Two thousand years later, in 1763, England's King George III issued a proclamation for similar reasons, forbidding American settlers to go beyond the crest of the Appalachian mountains. There was no wall to enforce the proclamation, though, so the colonists didn't pay much attention to the imaginary line.)

The Parthenon, built in Athens some two hundred years before the Great Wall, is a temple to the goddess Athena—specifically, to Athena Parthenos, or Athena the Virgin. It also harbored smaller shrines for the cults of other Greek deities. However, the motives behind its construction were mainly political, not religious.

After their city was sacked by the Persians in 480 B.C., the citizens of Athens took an oath that they would leave the ruined temples undisturbed, to remind future generations of the atrocities committed by their enemies. This "eternal" oath, however, lasted only thirty years. By then, Athens had made peace with Persia—and more importantly, the public treasury was full of money that had originally belonged to other Greek cities (it had been taken to Athens for safekeeping after the Persians were driven out, and was never returned).

The city's leader, Pericles, saw what any politician would see in a budget surplus: a golden opportunity for pork-barrel spending. In fact, Pericles had wanted to spend some of his personal fortune on a public construction program, to ensure that the ensuing positive sentiment would benefit him directly. But Athens had just enacted a law requiring that public works be financed exclusively with public funds, so Pericles proposed spending the budget surplus instead.

In addition to creating jobs (and votes for Pericles) at home, the centerpiece of the new program—the Parthenon—was a tool of Athenian foreign policy as well. It was no accident that the grandest building in all Greece was to be dedicated to the worship of Athena, the protector and patroness of the city of Athens. The message was obvious—Athens is the richest and most powerful city in the land—and was emphasized by statues and bas-relief sculptures throughout the building recounting the history of Athens's rise to greatness. There *were* religious services held there, but the building was meant to inspire devotion to the Athenian state as much as to the virgin goddess.

The Parthenon was built at least nominally for religious purposes, but in 1889, in Paris, "the new secular faith in material progress justified an engineering feat for its own sake," wrote Joseph Harris, historian of the Eiffel Tower. Just as the temple of Athena was a political as well as religious symbol, so the great Parisian tower was built, in Gustave Eiffel's own words, not only "to the glory of modern science" but also "to the greater honor of French industry."

England and France had been fighting, militarily and economically, for years. In the late nineteenth century, the battlefields of their cold war were the world's fairs in London and Paris. France also felt the need to erase the humiliation of its defeat in the Franco-Prussian war in 1871. The planners of the 1889 Paris fair wanted to showcase France's technological superiority by constructing a first: a thousand-foot tower. (The Washington Monument, completed in 1884, is only 555 feet high.)

A contest was held, and among the many rejected proposals were a monument in the shape of a guillotine to mark the hundredth anniversary of the revolution; a huge sprinkler to water the city during dry weather; and a tower with immense mirrors to light the "city of light" at night, as well as sickrooms near the top where patients could go to breathe clean air without traveling to the Alps. Eiffel, of course, won the contract, worth $300,000, and the rights to restaurant concessions on the tower for the next twenty years.

Not everyone approved. Composer Charles Gounod, writer Guy de Maupassant, painter A. W. Bouguereau, and other artists published an open letter containing the worst insult they could think of: "Even commercial America" wouldn't build such an ugly structure! There were technical objections, too: A math professor said the tower would collapse as soon as it reached 748 feet. (Engineers made similar objections to the design of architect Frank Lloyd Wright's "Fallingwater" house in the 1930s; they said it would collapse. Wright showed his disdain by burying the engineers' reports in the house's foundation. Fallingwater, like the Eiffel Tower, is still standing.)

On its completion, the tower held restaurants and tourist observation platforms. At its pinnacle was an apartment for Eiffel himself, as well as rooms for meterological data collection and scientific experiments. It became a favorite of stunt-performers: in 1891 a man walked up the stairs to the tower's 200-foot-high first platform on stilts; the first descent down the stairs from that platform on a bicycle took place in 1923, but we had to wait until 1958 for the considerably harder descent by unicycle. Before World War II, the tower was adorned with lights that gave the time, the temperature, and an ad for Citroën automobiles. The tower is now a popular suicide location, second only to the Golden Gate Bridge.

Gustave Eiffel didn't rest on his laurels and his $300,000. He went on to build the world's first wind tunnel in 1906 for research on airplane wings and propellers, and made some important aerodynamic discoveries. A few years later, Paris officials showed their gratitude to the designer of the city's most famous symbol: they cited his wind tunnel for violating zoning laws, forcing him to move it out of town.

Not-So-Mellow Yellow

You don't buy beer, you rent it. And like most things you rent, it's not in the same condition when you're finished with it as when you first got it. As the porter in *Macbeth* said, drink is a great provoker of three things: nose painting, sleep, and urine.

The precise makeup of urine depends on what you've been eating, drinking, or smoking, as all drug-testing labs know. But in general, urine is 98 percent water; most of the rest is urea (a product of the breakdown of amino acids in the body). It also contains calcium, phosphates, sodium—and ammonium, which doesn't stink but which soon decomposes into ammonia, causing that "stale-piss" smell in the rest rooms of places where they rent a lot of beer.

Although urea is the major ingredient (other than water) in human urine, it isn't found in the urine of any other mammal except the Dalmatian dog. Frogs' and fishes' urine has even more water in it than ours. Birds' urine, on the other hand, is thick: It's that white stuff that lands on your car.

For those into numbers: the pH of urine can vary anywhere from 4.7 to 8.0; it freezes anywhere from 27 to 31

133

degrees F., so it's a weak antifreeze; its specific gravity (weight relative to water) is about 1.02; and a typical person passes between two and three pints of urine a day—unless he's been renting a lot of beer, in which case all bets are off.

John Doe Versus Richard Roe

JUSTICE Grice of the Georgia Supreme Court rolled up his sleeves, breathed a heavy sigh, and began writing the opinion of the court: "Those litigious characters, John Doe and Richard Roe, are here again. . . ." That was in 1964. John Doe had indeed been in court again, and again, over and over, for three hundred years. He shows up less frequently now than he once did but often causes trouble and confusion when he does.

Like many of the quaint (some would say idiotic) oddities of English and American law, John Doe can trace his pedigree back to the days of knights in armor. Concepts from the feudal system governed English land law even after that system of lords and vassals had long been a thing of the past. Additionally, over time, legal procedures became increasingly strict and rigid. By the 1600s, a plaintiff whose specific problem didn't fit into one of the narrowly defined categories of lawsuits allowed by the courts couldn't even get a hearing.

Buying and selling land were rare in medieval times. The king theoretically owned all the land, and parceled it out to his chief vassals to use in return for a payment or service, such as recruiting knights for the royal army. By the seventeenth century, land transfers had become more common, but many bizarre and anachronistic procedures

135

remained in effect. Some landowners, for example, technically held their land under a grant from the lord of some manor or other, whose manorial court they had to attend regularly in order to keep their rights. Others still owed service or payment to the king in return for the use of their land: Charles I tried for a while to run the country with these feudal revenues alone, in an attempt to govern without Parliament (and hence without the taxes only Parliament can levy). And there was no easy way for a person to get into court to prove the simple fact that he owned a plot of land.

English lawyers, though, are very good at finding a roundabout way to a goal when no sensible, direct approach is available. Since the fourteenth century, there had existed a form of lawsuit called "ejectment." A person who was paying rent for some land, had tried to take possession of it, and had been thrown out by a squatter could bring an action of ejectment and recover damages. Unfortunately, because of the courts' strict rules, an ejectment suit was useless to someone trying to prove that he *owned* the land outright. Only a *renter* could bring the suit.

Around 1660, a bright lawyer (with the connivance of Chief Justice Rolle) devised a successful ploy. My client (the lawyer thought) needs to prove that he owns a property. He gets two friends together, writes out a lease to one of them, and then instructs the second one to throw the first one off the property. The evicted friend then sues the evictor under the principle of ejectment, and in order to prove that *he* was the rightful *lessee*, he must also prove that my *client* is the rightful *owner*, which is what we wanted in the first place.

At first, the "lessee" and "ejector" would actually go to the property in dispute and physically (but gently) push each other around for a few seconds, while cooperative witnesses looked on. Eventually, the two play-acting friends became unnecessary. The court would simply receive a complaint signed by "John Doe," claiming that he had rented some land but had been ejected from it by "Richard Roe." The suit, of course, was really filed by a behind-the-scenes plaintiff, the person actually claiming ownership of the land. Then the behind-the-scenes defendant would receive a letter from Richard Roe, asking him to come to court and help Roe defend himself. When "Roe's landlord" showed up at court, he was given a choice: either agree that the fictitious leases existed and that the alleged ejection had taken place, and proceed with the trial on the real issue of who owned the land—or forfeit the suit immediately.

The *Doe* v. *Roe* gimmick was made obsolete and unnecessary in Britain by an act of parliament in 1852. Some American states hung on to it for another century, however, which brings us back to Justice Grice and his two "litigious characters."

To leave Messrs. Doe and Roe out of it for a moment, the real issue before the Georgia court in 1964 was a dispute between two families over ownership of a tenth of an acre of land that blocked a driveway. They brought the case before a jury under the old English action of ejectment, which was still valid in Georgia at the time. The jury decided in favor of the plaintiffs. On appeal, however, the verdict was overturned because the plaintiffs had failed to allege that they had assigned a (fictitious) lease to the (fictitious) John Doe—though their lawyer could have amended the papers and made such a claim right up to the moment the verdict was delivered. The case had to be retried.

One of the lawyers in the Georgia case later wrote that the defendants had been "clutching at straws" in their appeal and were "fortunate to confuse the issue and secure a reversal." The second trial ended in a mistrial, but on the third attempt the defendants finally won, thanks to John Doe.

Doe's legal career sprang from a strange twist of medieval land law, but he appears in other kinds of cases as well. In England, a plaintiff used to have to produce two sureties (people who would guarantee to pay any court costs that might be levied against him if he were to lose) before he could file a suit. When such fees became obsolete, the signatures of two sureties were still required, but the courts allowed lawyers to put down the names John Doe and Richard Roe.

Doe and Roe are often used when pseudonyms are necessary to protect someone's privacy, as in the abortion case of *Roe* v. *Wade*. There is also something called a John Doe arrest warrant, but it doesn't necessarily specify that name; it's a warrant for the arrest of a person whose name is unknown but who can be identified by physical description or address. In another vein, the state of Virginia requires automobile-insurance policies to include an uninsured-motorist clause, and then allows an injured driver to sue his own insurance company, specifying the defendant as John Doe, if the other driver can't be found. The insurance company has the same kind of choice as the defendant in the old English ejectment cases: either pay up immediately, or come to court and defend that litigious character John Doe.

The Strange Career of Dr. Drew's Death

The New York Times told the story. The *Encyclopaedia Brittanica* told the story. *Time* magazine told the story. Even that trustworthy doctor played by Alan Alda in *M*A*S*H* told the story of Dr. Charles Drew, a famous blood-plasma researcher, who was injured in a car crash in North Carolina in 1950 and bled to death after being turned away from a hospital emergency room because he was black.

All these distinguished authorities have told the story. But the story isn't true.

The other three passengers in Drew's car—all of them medical doctors, and all of them black—have repeatedly explained what happened on the night of April 1, 1950. They say that Drew fell asleep at the wheel; they had an accident; Drew was seriously injured; an ambulance took him to the nearest hospital (Alamance General, in Burlington, N.C.); the first doctor to see him, Dr. Harold Kernodle, knew of Drew's research and recognized him immediately; three of the hospital's physicians did their best to save Drew's life, but the injuries were too severe and he died in the hospital without regaining consciousness.

One of the passengers, Dr. John Ford, wrote in 1971: "The statement about his bleeding to death because of refusal of treatment is utterly false." Another, Dr. Walter

139

Johnson, wrote in 1982: "There was no evidence to suggest that Dr. Drew received less than acceptable emergency treatment." The third passenger, Dr. Samuel Bullock, and a former student of Drew's, Dr. Charles Quick, who was at the hospital that night, have also debunked the rumor.

A similar rumor, also false, was spread about the death in 1937 of blues singer Bessie Smith. Of course it is true that patients *have* been turned away from hospitals because of their race, but Dr. Charles Drew was not one of them.

Racial discrimination didn't kill Drew, but it did affect his professional career. He never could become a member of the American Medical Association, because the local chapter in his hometown of Washington, D.C., had a whites-only policy until 1952. And even though Drew was the medical director of a large blood bank in the early days of World War II, he himself was unable to donate blood because the armed forces, the main consumer of blood products, would not accept donations from nonwhites. (In 1942 the policy changed, but donated blood was still kept segregated by race.)

Drew's contribution to medical science is also often misunderstood. He did not make any astounding new discoveries or epochal breakthroughs. He did, however, *synthesize* and *apply* the work of many other scientists in unprecedented ways. Perhaps his greatest accomplishment was the massive "Blood for Britain" program in 1940, which supplied American blood plasma to British forces fighting the Nazis, at a time when Britain lacked the technology to process blood products on such a large scale. Drew's development of techniques for processing, preserving, and shipping huge amounts of blood products came just in time to be vital to the Allied war effort and has helped save countless lives since then in peacetime as well.

Who Invented
the Wheel?

"**D**ON'T reinvent the wheel" is a metaphor meaning "avoid redundant [and therefore wasted] creativity." Of course, no one would *literally* reinvent the wheel today. But what about ancient peoples? How many of them really did reinvent the wheel, not aware of its existence elsewhere? Apparently, none—but long after its invention, in a large part of the world the wheel was *deinvented* and fell out of use for centuries.

The best guess of archaeologists and historians is that the wheel as a means of transport was invented once and for all by someone in or near Uruk, Mesopotamia (now Warka, Iraq), sometime before 3000 B.C. From there it spread rapidly, both because it was useful and because, by making long-distance travel easier, it provided the means for its own quick diffusion. Wheeled vehicles were in use in India before 2000 B.C. and in Egypt and China before 1000 B.C.

It's virtually impossible for any five thousand-year-old wooden wheels to have survived, so researchers have had to use other evidence to deduce the origin and dissemination of the wheel. The bones of castrated oxen found in the ruins of an ancient city, for example, are a good sign that cattle were being used to pull wheeled vehicles. (The bones of a castrated animal grow differently from those of

141

a nonneutered one, and the two can be distinguished even after the rest of the body has disappeared.)

Surprisingly, after centuries of use throughout Asia, Europe, and the Mediterranean area, the wheel disappeared from Persia (present-day Iran) and the Arab world sometime between A.D. 200 and 700. Again, much of the early evidence is indirect: For example, linguists have pointed to the absence from the Persian language of words relating to wheeled vehicles at the time of the Arab conquest of Persia in A.D. 640. Well documented, however, is the lack of wheeled transport throughout the Islamic world during the Middle Ages and up to the eighteenth century.

Why would an entire culture deinvent the wheel? Politics, mainly. Nomadic peoples who relied on camels for transportation began to wrest power from city-dwelling and agricultural societies in the Middle East a few hundred years before Mohammed's time. They invented a high-technology military device—a camel saddle useful in combat—that gave them the advantage in battle. The nomads' victories gave them control over highly profitable trading routes, which they exploited with camel caravans. Since camels were becoming the exclusive means of long-distance hauling, they began to be used within cities as well. The camel-breeding nomads encouraged this trend, since it increased the market for their livestock, and the relative scarcity of wood in desert countries accelerated the move away from wheeled vehicles.

European influence on Persia and the Arab countries led to the reintroduction of the wheel in more recent times, but historian Richard W. Bulliet, author of *The Camel and the Wheel*, says there is still an "unconscious prejudice against wheeled vehicles" in the Middle East. Wheelbarrows, for example, are used on almost every construction site in the U.S. but rarely in Iran. Centuries of wheellessness have left their mark on Middle Eastern societies: Cities there are less centrally planned, and less geometrically laid out, than in other parts of the world. (Compare, for example, the narrow, winding alleyways of Casablanca with the broad, grid-patterned streets of Washington.)

The fact that the Indians of North and South America never invented the wheel is sometimes, erroneously, offered as evidence of backwardness or cultural inferiority. Actually, many ancient American societies knew of the wheel, though they used it only on children's toys. It wasn't stupidity that kept them from using wheeled carts for transportation; it was simple lack of necessity. Some Americans had domesticated animals, such as the llama and alpaca, to carry loads for them. A sure-footed pack animal is much more useful in rugged terrain (like the Andes mountains) than wheels. And if the Indians had built wheeled carts, what would have pulled them? There were no horses and no domesticated cattle in pre-Columbian America. Their methods of transportation served the Americans well until they encountered the colonizing Europeans. Then their lack of the wheel turned out to be a severe military disadvantage.

What Causes Cold Headaches?

Every summer, you remember not to gulp that milk shake or frozen margarita so fast. Unfortunately, you probably remember that only *after* you've gotten a painful "cold headache."

Doctors now know what causes the "cold" or "ice-cream" headache. But pity the poor patient who volunteered for the experiment! Researchers used "a subject in whom it was possible to examine separate parts of the esophagus, stomach, and mouth"—in other words, he was already split open from guggle to zatch for some surgical procedure. They held ice against various parts of his innards. The patient didn't have any problem with ice in his stomach or esophagus, but ice on the roof of the mouth caused a headache. This let the doctors know exactly which nerves are responsible for the pain.

This experiment might sound like a candidate for one of those "Golden Fleece" awards that ignorant politicians give to scientists whose research seems expensive and pointless. But a cold headache can be more serious that just a temporary annoyance for hot and thirsty summertime beachgoers. Polio patients getting air through a nasal tube often suffered from headaches until doctors noticed that the air was being humidified—and cooled. When the air was warmed, the patients' headaches disappeared.

The Etiquette of Ejection

THE most complicated thing a fighter pilot has to learn about his ejector seat isn't how to use it. It's the etiquette he has to follow *after* he uses it.

For example, here is the drill a navy pilot is supposed to follow after he bails out and is rescued:

• Give a bottle of liquor to the person who packed his parachute and to each crewman of the rescue helicopter.
• Cut the parachute up into scarves for fellow officers.
• Buy a tub of ice cream for the crew of the destroyer or submarine involved in the rescue.

It's not all give and no take for the ejected flyer, however: He gets what the navy calls "a suitable portion of medicinal alcohol" prescribed by the flight surgeon; and he becomes a member of the Irvin Parachute Company's Caterpillar Club (named for the worms from whose silk the earliest parachutes were made).

The ejector seat was developed after World War II and was first tested by volunteers over the Pacific. The first emergency use of an ejector seat was by navy Lt. Jack Fruin, who lost control of his plane while performing in an air show in South Carolina in 1949. He bailed out at thirty thousand feet, hit the water, and was injured, but survived.

Most ejector seats work at any altitude—pilots have even bailed out safely on the runway during takeoff. Some newer ejector seats, however, blast the pilot *down* instead of up, and some have been killed when they apparently forgot what kind of seat they were using and bailed out at low altitudes like three hundred feet.

According to a (possibly apocryphal) story told in air force circles, it's even possible to eject from a plane that's stock-still on the ground, as an air force ROTC cadet supposedly did during training. She flew up into the air and fell onto the wing of the aircraft. After she got out of the hospital, the air force billed her $2,000 for damage to the plane. Why did she pull the lever in a plane that wasn't even moving? She thought she had heard the command, "Bail out! Bail out! Bail out!" through her headphones, but in fact all the instructor had said was, "Are you securely buckled in?"

"A Potpourri of Nematodes" or, As the Worm Turns

If you wake up in the middle of the night and a foot-long worm with three lips is squiggling out of your nostril, don't be alarmed. In particular, don't gasp, because you might choke on it.

No, this isn't a useless piece of trivia about a bizarre, rare disease. Worms like this infest a billion people all over the world, including millions in the United States. They can cause widespread malnutrition, they can kill people, and they can ravage a nation's economy as profoundly as a depression or drought.

Many species of worms infest human beings, most of them very small. But in the foot-long category, the primary candidates are the Ascaris and the Guinea worm.

The Ascaris spends most of its time in the intestines, but it has to go through quite an ordeal to get there safely. Victims usually pick up the worm by swallowing its eggs on unwashed vegetables. (A parasitology graduate student in New York almost killed his roommates in 1970 by secretly putting Ascaris eggs into their breakfast.) The eggs have been found in other places too, including paper money. They hatch in the upper intestines, but for some reason the baby worms don't stay there. Instead, they invade the bloodstream, migrate to the lungs, slither up the windpipe, and are swallowed again. If they survive their bath in stomach acid, they wind up in the intestine again, where they can grow as long as eighteen inches.

The worms' odyssey through the host's body seems to serve no useful purpose and, in fact, is dangerous to the worms as well as to the host. Many worms go astray during their migration, get stranded in hostile territory, die, and cause inflammations. The long trip may be a now-useless holdover from an earlier stage in the worms' evolution: It's thought that their distant ancestors perhaps had to infest an intermediate host, or pass through the skin of their ultimate victim, in order to trigger certain growth processes in their own bodies. For their distant offspring, the Ascaris worms, a journey through the human body may simulate these events of the ancestors' life cycle.

The worms who survive to maturity feed on the liquid contents of the gut, sometimes causing malnutrition in the human host. If they overpopulate, they may become a knotted mass that blocks the intestine, killing the host; or some may penetrate the intestinal wall, leading to a life-threatening abdominal infection.

When they're not eating, the worms are driven to reproduce. Female worms will wander around if there are no males nearby. ("A similar restlessness," one team of parasite researchers wryly noted, "can be observed in even higher forms of animals.") If a worm travels from the intestines into the stomach, it may thrash around and nauseate its host. Or it may continue up the esophagus, eventually coming out the nose or mouth. Parasitologists have variously described the result as "chagrin and embarrassment" and "a predictable consternation."

U.S. senator Allen Ellender of Louisiana was predictably consternated as a child, around the year 1900, when Ascaris worms came out of his mouth. A reporter said that Ellender "appeared nonplussed" when he learned, at a Senate Hunger Committee hearing in 1969, that in his home state there were still many people infested by the parasite. Even today, the southeastern U.S. is one of many areas of epidemic infestation.

Pigs as well as people suffer from the Ascaris worm. "This is not surprising," says one parasitology textbook, "since the physiologies of people and swine are remarkably similar, as on occasion, are their eating and social habits."

The Guinea worm's mode of infestation isn't quite as disgusting as that of the Ascaris, but it can get under your skin—literally. It causes blisters, pain, and fever, and it's most likely to attack at seasons when agricultural labor is most needed. Guinea worms may put half the local population out of work for weeks, and sometimes cause permanent joint damage.

The familiar symbol of medicine, the caduceus (a snake wrapping itself around a pole), is thought to have been inspired by an ancient treatment for Guinea worms. The blister in which the worm lives is punctured, and the worm is wound around a stick. The stick is twisted a little bit each day so that another inch of the worm is pulled out. It can take weeks to get the whole worm, but extracting it too forcefully can break it, which can lead to serious infection.

The Bible contains an ancient, though garbled, description of Guinea worm extraction in the Book of Numbers. The Israelites were bitten by "fiery serpents . . . And the Lord said unto Moses, Make thee a fiery serpent, and set it upon a pole: and it shall come to pass, that every one that is bitten, when he looketh upon it, shall live." Modern researchers point out that Guinea worms are common in the Middle East and that, according to the biblical account, there had been a drought, probably leading to the formation of stagnant pools of water—the perfect breeding ground for the Guinea worm.

The World Health Organization is mounting an international campaign to eradicate Guinea worm disease. Former president Jimmy Carter projects that it could be wiped out in India by 1991 and universally by 1995 if the campaign is adequately funded. The governments of India, Nigeria, and other countries where the worm devastates health and the economy are cooperating with industrialized countries, UNICEF, the Carter Center, and other organizations to teach people in affected areas how to avoid the worm. Even today, some people think infestation is due to evil spirits. In fact, the worm can be avoided by boiling or filtering drinking water or switching from ponds to wells as water sources. The American Cyanamid Co. has donated $2 million worth of its Abate brand larvacide to the effort—enough to remove the worm completely from drinking water in the worst-affected African countries. If the campaign succeeds, Guinea worm infestation will be the first disease to be wiped out since smallpox in 1970.

Of the smaller worms that can infest people, the one that causes trichinosis is well known, as is the fact that it can be ingested in undercooked pork. But other exotic meats, such as bear, can also carry the parasite. One West African researcher tells of some foreign visitors in Senegal who contracted trichinosis from eating warthog—"an obvious act of indiscretion in the tropics," said the doctor, "or anywhere else for that matter!"

Early Electricity

Say you're an eighties kind of guy—1880s, that is. You're into high tech, and you want to be the first person on your block to have this great new invention in your home: electric light. You should probably take a few tips from the tycoon William H. Vanderbilt on how it should *not* be done.

Vanderbilt spent a small fortune on electric light and generated a calamity. In 1881, he had his New York City mansion wired for hundreds of lamps, but then discovered that the central power station was too far away to deliver enough current to run the lights. So he had a generator built in the basement. The first day it was turned on, a short circuit started a fire. Vanderbilt had the generator removed and went back to gas lighting.

Even those who were luckier than Vanderbilt and successfully electrified their homes had big bills to pay. The power itself was never very expensive, but the first incandescent bulbs, with bamboo filaments, cost $5 apiece and burned out after only a couple of hundred hours. (The price fell to 20 cents by 1894.) They also had to buy sockets, fixtures, fuses, and the like.

And that's where the plot thickened. Thomas Edison invented the first commercially practical light bulb—that itself was the work of a genius—but he didn't stop there.

Edison didn't want to be a mere genius; he wanted to be a *rich* genius. So he went on to invent and patent all the hardware and paraphernalia necessary for installing and using his bulbs.

Edison's company also sold the necessary electric power in many cities. There had been electric companies before Edison's, but their customers were a small number of factories and stores that used industrial-strength arc lights, which were far too bright for home use. Edison's bulb was the first practical electric light for home and office, and his electric company's salesmen went door to door singing its praises and signing up customers.

Electricity in those days was 110 volts, about the same as ours is today, because that was the most efficient voltage for the type of wires Edison used. But it was DC (direct current), not the AC (alternating current) we're familiar with.

It was Westinghouse, Edison's chief competitor, who pioneered the use of AC, and the battle between the two kinds of current was literally deadly. When the state of New York abandoned the gallows for the electric chair in 1890, Edison connived with officials to have a Westinghouse AC generator installed at the prison to effect the killing. He apparently hoped that this sick publicity stunt would turn people off on AC.* But in the long run, AC proved to be more useful for industrial purposes than DC and eventually became the standard in the United States.

President Benjamin Harrison apparently thought neither AC nor DC safe. During the renovation of the decrepit old White House in 1891, electric lights were installed—but the president and first lady never touched the light switches themselves, for fear of shock. Whenever they wanted the lights turned on or off, they called

---

*The story of this execution, and Edison's part in it, are the basis of Christopher Davis's novel *A Peep into the Twentieth Century.*

a servant. They kept the gas lights, too, which made it impossible to wire the White House the usual way, by running wires through the old gas pipes. Instead, the walls had to be ripped out for the wires to be installed, at great expense.

Monks apparently had more faith in electricity than skittish secular politicians did. The year 1895 saw the world's first all-electric monastery, near Niagara Falls. The monks used electricity for heating, cooking, and doing laundry. But even these futuristic friars still used candles in the chapel.

Grenades: An Explosion of Technology

Here's the brilliant idea of someone in the U.S. Army at the beginning of World War II: Every red-blooded American boy knows how to throw a baseball, right? So if only we could develop a hand grenade the same size, shape, and weight as a baseball, we wouldn't have to waste time teaching soldiers how to throw them.

But designers couldn't make a perfectly round grenade—there has to be some kind of pin or trigger on the outside to activate the thing. Besides, no one seems to have considered that in a war you rarely have a chance to stand on a mound, rub a rosin bag, spit tobacco juice, get signals from the catcher, take careful aim, and pitch one right over the enemy's home plate.

Armies have used grenades throughout this century, so it's hard to believe that an 1880s British military manual said grenades were an old-fashioned weapon that wouldn't be used in wars of the future. Those nineteenth-century experts, however, weren't as wrong as they now sound. Back then, *grenade* meant a big, black round bomb with a burning fuse sticking out of it—the kind of bomb that cartoon character Boris Badenov is always throwing at Rocky and Bullwinkle. These old grenades, invented five hundred years ago, were almost as dangerous to their throwers as to the enemy, so other soldiers deeply respected the brave grenadiers who used them.

Soldiers in World War I, the first wholesale users of modern grenades, were almost as much at risk as their medieval ancestors. The bombs were mounted on long sticks, to give the throwers more leverage, and exploded on impact. Unfortunately, they often hit the side of a trench during the thrower's backswing, killing him and his comrades. Engineers went back to the drawing boards.

The grenade as we know it today is essentially the same as the "Mills bomb," invented in England in 1915. It's an egg-shaped device with grooves that give it a pineapple-like appearance. A pin holds a curved lever in place against the outside of the grenade. The thrower pulls the pin and releases the lever, setting off a spring-activated fuse inside the grenade. If he decides not to throw the bomb before releasing the lever, he can always reinsert the pin. But as soon as he lets go the lever, he has only about five seconds before the grenade explodes.

For many years it was commonly thought, even among the military, that the grooves on the outside of the grenade made it break up into pieces of equal size. But apparently the inventor put them there simply to give the soldier a better grip. In fact, the old Mills bomb usually *didn't* break up along the grooves. You have to put the grooves on the *inside* of a grenade to make it blow up uniformly; modern grenades use this construction. This is important because the thrower needs to know how far he must toss the bomb in order to be safe from the explosion. If the grenade didn't break up into equal-size pieces, the smaller fragments could travel up to two hundred yards and injure the thrower.

Science marches on: a Dutch weapons firm has recently developed a golf-ball-size grenade that can be thrown a hundred yards and kills anyone within ten yards of the explosion but is harmless beyond fifteen yards.

Josiah Wedgwood: Potter, Scientist, Businessman, Jerk

Wedgwood: The name brings to mind pastel-blue plates with white bas-relief figures, nostalgia for days gone by, soothing images of gracious living and Grandma's house.

Josiah Wedgwood himself, though, was far less pleasant. Born in 1730, Wedgwood was a modern manufacturer and a scientist rolled into one. In his pottery business, he was determined to break the old apprentice-journeyman system, in which craftsmen learned a whole trade. Instead, like Henry Ford many years after him, he employed workers at narrowly specialized jobs. For instance, he hired some as "stewkers," who did nothing but make handles for jugs. This molded workers into efficient machines on an assembly line, and made it harder for them to take their talents elsewhere or go into business for themselves. The minimal skills required for each specialized job also reduced each worker's power to bargain: A worker might threaten to quit, but Wedgwood could easily replace him.

Then the American Revolution disrupted the economy of Britain. Unemployment rose and wages fell. There were even some modern-style strikes, and at Wedgwood's works there was a riot. Wedgwood lectured the workers, telling them to seek their goals by peaceful means (even though, in the past, those who had peacefully asked for raises had often been fired, and his workers' wages hardly increased at all between 1762 and 1790). He even took the Big Brother–like step of encouraging his employees' children to inform on parents who engaged in protests.

In addition to intimidating the less-skilled workers, Wedgwood was concerned with keeping other employees from going to America or France and taking his trade secrets with them. But instead of wooing them with higher pay, he frightened them with exaggerated stories of storm and shipwreck on the Atlantic Ocean and unemployment and oppression in France.

Wedgwood was apparently no worse an employer than most other English capitalists of his day. That isn't saying much, but he did have some redeeming qualities.

Ironically, this man who was probably regarded as a slave driver by many of his employees was a political opponent of the slave trade. Josiah Wedgwood himself designed the famous logo of the British Society for the Suppression of the Slave Trade: a picture of a black man wearing chains and saying, "Am I not a man and a brother?"

Wedgwood was one of the first industrialists to put much effort into research and development. He was a good friend of the chemist Joseph Priestly, and corresponded with other scientists, including Antoine Lavoisier and Benjamin Franklin. He kept meticulous records of his experiments with different materials and methods of making his products, and—the hallmark of the modern scientific method—he made sure the experiments were reproducible.

When it came to his health, Wedgwood was something of a crank. He rode on horseback ten to twenty miles a day (which is good exercise), but also ate a diet that included egg yolks, rhubarb, and soap. He died at the age of sixty-five.

Tornado Pranks

TORNADOES at their most violent have winds of three to six hundred miles per hour. (Scientists disagree on the exact figure for top wind speed, which is impossible to measure directly.) Usually, the forces of a tornado simply explode or crush everything in the whirlwind's path, but sometimes they play almost incredible "pranks." Some documented examples:

• A wooden beam was driven through a tree, and chickens lost their feathers but were otherwise unhurt (1860, Midwest).

• A tree lost its bark but was otherwise undamaged; geese were stripped of their feathers, which were found in a bunch in a nearby fence (1883, Illinois).

• The roof of a house was torn off and a child was lifted out, fell six blocks away, and survived (1890, Louisville).

• A two-by-four was driven through a ⅝-inch-thick steel plate; a man driving a team of horses lost his horses, but he and his wagon were not harmed (1896, St. Louis).

• A tornado sucked the shoes off the corpses of several victims; one person lost the hair from his head but was not injured; and feathers were plucked off only one side of a chicken (1905, Midwest).

• A bean was driven halfway through an eggshell; the fit was so tight, the egg was not leaking (1951, Nebraska).

America: Number One (and Number Two) in Space

AالسTRONAUTS are our heroes. They endure years of rigorous training, risk their lives, and make important scientific discoveries. But perhaps the thing for which they most deserve our admiration and respect is this: They have to go to the bathroom in zero gravity.

Relieving oneself in today's space shuttle is a civilized affair compared to the hardships of earlier space missions. Conservative senators will be glad to know that there are no unisex toilets on the shuttle, nosirree: There are separate men's and ladies' rooms. The toilets are equipped with foot restraints and seat belts, and are flushed with air rather than water. Nevertheless, they are much more akin to earth commodes than those that their predecessors, the Apollo astronauts, had to put up with.

In the first years of space exploration, reporters invariably told the public about the astronauts' 5:00 A.M. breakfast of steak and eggs. The menu was not solely intended to give the astronauts a tasty and nourishing bon voyage repast. In fact, it was the same fare they had been eating for weeks. The items were selected less for their nutritional value than for their lack of fiber. Especially on flights of several days, it was important to reduce the amount of residue in the intestines so the astronauts would spend as little time as possible evacuating their bowels. Before his

159

historic lunar flight, Neil Armstrong told his wife that he was sick of steak after having had to eat it day after day for several weeks.

During launch, and for the first several hours of the flight, Apollo astronauts had to wear a pressure suit. Inside was a fecal containment bag (fancy NASA jargon for a diaper) and a special condom hooked up to a tube and bottle. The diaper was usually not needed but was a precaution in case an emergency forced the astronauts to leave their pressure suits on for a day or two.

If things were going well, the astronauts could take off their space suits during most of the trip and avail themselves of a relatively conventional urinal located in a closed compartment. Solid waste, however, was another problem entirely.

Astronauts had to defecate into a bag. And according to Charles Duke of Apollo 16, it didn't really work very well. Unless the material was quite solid, it was hard to catch it all in the bag; this problem reached horrendous proportions when Ron Evans of the Apollo 17 crew came down with the space traveler's trots on the return voyage.

After getting everything under control in the bag, the astronaut had to knead the bag until an inner sac, containing an antiseptic, ruptured and mixed with the contents. This disinfection was a precaution in case the bags sprang a leak during the flight.

All the fecal bags were brought back to earth for scientific study. NASA has published a complete list of each and every one of these items: whom it came from, the date and time, and the weight.

Although the astronauts' diet was supposed to reduce the waste problem, the kind of water they drank during the flight made it worse. Apollo's fuel cells manufactured drinking water as a by-product but didn't filter out all the hydrogen gas bubbles, which cause flatulence. Buzz Aldrin joked that on Apollo 11's trip back from the moon, the astronauts thought about turning off the spaceship's thruster rockets and using their own jet propulsion instead.

On Apollo flights, liquid waste was dumped overboard, but it tended to vaporize and form a cloud of droplets that surrounded and followed the spacecraft and obscured the astronauts' view. They had to be careful not to dump any liquid right before they had an important observation or photograph scheduled.

After the Apollo program ended in 1972, engineers continued to devote a lot of work to the problem of space waste. On long space-station missions it wouldn't be economical to keep dumping scarce water overboard in the form of urine, for example. Besides, long-term residents of space probably wouldn't put up with the time-consuming and disgusting procedure of squishing their own excrement around in a plastic bag.

After years of research and development, space engineers came up with a much more acceptable zero-g toilet, which they dubbed Super John. Short blasts of air separate any dangling feces from the astronaut's body (Gemini crew members had to use a finger in a glove). More drafts of air flush everything away into the bowels, so to speak, of the spacecraft's plumbing system. A "slinger" separates liquid from solid waste. Water is reclaimed from the urine. The rest is centrifuged onto the inside of a cylinder, where it's baked for hours until it's dry and sterile. The air, too, is purified and returned to the cabin for breathing.

Fortunately, we ordinary earthlings don't have to take recycling quite to that extreme—at least, not yet.

Archimedes: Merchant of Death

THE ancient Greek mathematician Archimedes is most famous for something he never did: jumping out of the bath and running naked through the streets shouting "Eureka!" after thinking of the answer to a physics problem. Less well known—but, unlike the "Eureka!" story, true—is that he was the first scientist to apply his knowledge to building weapons of war.

Archimedes lived in Syracuse, a Greek city-state on the island of Sicily, in the third century B.C. The ruler, King Hieron (who was Archimedes's cousin), was interested in the mathematician's work and asked him to put some of his theories to practical use. In response, Archimedes improved some old weapons and invented new ones.

Using mathematics and physics, he made catapults more accurate. One of his inventions, the "scorpion," made it possible to destroy buildings and ships from the inside without having to breach the walls or hulls first, by precisely aiming burning projectiles at windows and portholes.

His most terrifying invention, though, was an entirely new weapon. With a crane mounted on a cliff overlooking the ocean, defenders could pick up the prow of an attacking ship, shake the sailors out, and drop the ship on the rocks below.

162

Not long after their invention, Archimedes had a chance to use some of these weapons against the Romans, who had decided to make Syracuse part of their empire. Archimedes's machines held off the attackers for some time—the sailors were particularly afraid of the ship-lifting crane—but eventually the city fell.

The Roman commander Marcellus knew of Archimedes's work, admired the man, and wanted to meet him. He gave strict orders that Archimedes was not to be harmed. But an ignorant Roman soldier killed him anyway—and was charged with murder when Marcellus found out about it.

Although Archimedes wrote many books on geometry and physics, he never published the plans for his weapons. Like so many scientists after him, he wanted to be remembered for his theoretical work, not for the destructive ends to which it was put.

Weird Legal Defenses

Most law schools push their students through a rigorous curriculum of contract, property, and constitutional law, civil and criminal procedure, and torts and courts and rules of all sorts. Sounds boring. Fortunately, our Last Resort Law School dispenses with all that, and offers only practical courses like this one: Weird but Useful Legal Defenses for Clients Who Can't Get off the Hook Any Other Way.

(Our own lawyers made us insert the following: This book is not a substitute for licensed legal advice. Do not try to use these defenses yourself. Void where taxed or prohibited. At participating dealers only. Your mileage may vary.)

Drunkenness has a commonly misunderstood effect on a criminal charge. Many people assume that drunkenness aggravates the offender's position. Others may have heard that intoxication is a defense against any accusation. The actual legal rule is more complicated than either statement.

The bare-bones rule is: Voluntary intoxication is usually not a broad defense, but it *can* be used as evidence to negate specific (not general) criminal intent. (More about those technical legal terms later.) In practice it means, for example, that a rip-roaring drunk who kills someone may

164

be acquitted of first-degree murder but convicted of manslaughter. Why? Because the definition of first-degree murder includes premeditation, which a drunk person may not be capable of. However, manslaughter is defined as requiring not premeditation but merely recklessness. The law considers getting drunk to be a reckless act, but pre-*medication* is not pre*meditation*.

The distinction between general and specific criminal intent was devised largely in response to the drunkenness defense. The original principle, that being drunk is no excuse, was laid down before alcoholism and addiction were widely accepted as diseases. Judges hate to abandon an old rule of law, so instead they punched it full of loopholes and exceptions. However, it's tough to use these exceptions successfully: a defendant has to prove he was *very* tanked to negate specific intent, the jury may not buy the excuse, and even then, the result is usually conviction on a lesser offense.

A 1955 Chicago kidnapping illustrates the difficulties arising in these cases. A woman spontaneously "adopted" two babies from strollers on a sidewalk and carried them to her home, where police found them during a house-to-house search. After her arrest, she claimed that she'd been so drunk she hadn't known what she was doing. However, there was evidence that she had bathed and fed the children, from which the court deduced that she hadn't been *sufficiently* hammered to use the defense, and she was convicted. Similarly, in 1975, a New Jersey court convicted a man of both drunk driving and receiving a stolen vehicle. The unlucky defendant was too tipsy to drive legally but not smashed enough to lack the specific intent to drive a car that didn't belong to him. Pennsylvania has forbidden the use of the intoxication defense altogether, except for reducing a first-degree murder charge to a lesser offense.

On the other hand, consider a couple of instances in which escaped and recaptured prisoners had their escape convictions overturned on appeal because they had been drunk at the time. In one case, a prisoner fooled guards by putting a dummy in his bed and hiding in the back of a truck. Unfortunately for him, he got snockered, went to sleep, and was discovered before the truck was driven out of the prison. The appeals court ruled that the jury should at least have been allowed to decide whether the prisoner, because of his drunkenness, lacked the "specific intent" to escape. In the other instance, a man walked away from a minimum-security prison to see his wife, who had threatened to leave him, but passed out on the way and fell into a mill pond, from which he was rescued by workers. In the judge's words, he "appeared to be a mobile mass of mud in which were set visible eyeballs," and was "falling-down drunk." His conviction for escape was also reversed on specific-intent grounds.

Involuntary intoxication is something else again. Some courts *do* recognize narcotics addiction, or side effects of legal prescription drugs, as a defense to criminal charges. So far, however, they don't accept *alcohol* addiction alone as a defense; there must be a particular claim of intoxication during the commission of the crime, and it has only a mitigating, not exculpating, effect.

Amnesia, a popular plot device in movies and TV shows, is not usually a valid legal defense, even if it is unquestionably legitimate and even if it makes it difficult for the defendant to assist his or her lawyer. (This rule was applied, for example, in the Patty Hearst case.) The defendant's memory is only one source of evidence, and the defense can build its case on witnesses, documents, and circumstantial evidence instead. However, if the amnesia is so profound that it prevents the lawyer from preparing a case at all, the court may rule that the defendant is incompetent to stand trial. The Kentucky Supreme Court came up with a novel approach to the problem: in that state, the prosecution must throw its files wide open to the defense if the accused is suffering from amnesia.

Multiple personality, another favorite of scriptwriters, is also tenuous as a defense. A woman arrested for drunk driving in Ohio in the 1980s claimed that her secondary personality, Jennifer, was in control at the time, having emerged because she had just learned that she had a lump in her breast. Jennifer, said the court, is "impulsive, angry, fearful, and anxious [and] has a drinking problem," unlike the woman's primary personality, but her three-faces-of-Eve defense was nevertheless rejected.

A defendant stands a slightly better chance pleading unconsciousness. The law presumes that if a person is *acting* as if he were conscious then he *is* conscious. But the defendant need only raise a reasonable doubt as to his consciousness in order for a jury to find him not guilty, in most states. Lawyers have used evidence of epilepsy, and of profound shock caused by attempted rape, in successful unconsciousness defenses.

There are, of course, many other legal defenses that don't depend on the psychiatric or chemical status of the defendant's brain. Most people have used this one, though not necessarily in court: "But Mom, all the other kids do it!" The courts agree with Mom—that's no excuse! Sometimes, though, if *public officials* are responsible for establishing a tradition, people are allowed to rely on their behavior, even if the law says otherwise. For example, it was customary in the 1940s in Mercer, Pennsylvania, for the sheriff to issue *two* witness summonses, one to compel appearance before a grand jury investigating a crime and a separate summons for the ensuing trial. When one witness received only the grand-jury summons and then didn't show up at the trial, he was prosecuted as an "absconding witness." The conviction was overturned because of the two-summons tradition. The rule isn't universal, though: A Washington, D.C., restaurant owner was prosecuted for racial discrimination in the 1950s under an almost century-old civil rights law, and his conviction was upheld even though the owner complained that the law had almost never been enforced against similar violators in the past.

Finally, consider the legal implications of the BEWARE OF DOG sign. We don't want to discourage anyone from posting such a sign if it will protect innocent passersby. But if the dog bites someone, the sign may actually hurt the dog owner's case in court. The rule isn't hard and fast, but if a bite victim can prove that the owner knew his dog was vicious—and the posting of a warning sign is evidence that he knew—the victim usually has an easier time collecting damages. Anyone who posts a BEWARE OF DOG sign thinking it will shield him from dog-bite lawsuits is barking up the wrong tree.

Dirt Eaters

Humorist Roy Blount, Jr., got so tired of Yankees asking him why all southerners eat dirt that he began handing out recipes for such alleged southern delicacies as "blackened red dirt." It isn't true that all southerners, or all members of any other ethnic group, eat dirt; however, the practice *has* been observed in many societies. It is most frequent among one particular *age* group: children between one and three.

Eating dirt is also called *geophagy,* from the Greek for "earth-eating." It is one form of what doctors call pica, which refers to the eating of any inappropriate item. (*Pica* is the Latin word for "magpie," a bird that will put just about anything into its mouth.)

Ancient writers mentioned geophagy, and thought it was especially prevalent among pregnant women. For centuries, doctors thought geophagy was the body's response to some nutritional deficiency. A person lacking iron, for example, would get an urge to eat something containing iron—even dirt. But no scientific study has ever proved this belief, and today doctors point to psychological causes for geophagy instead.

Some of these new theories are plausible, though some are contradictory. One theory holds that young children are free of adult food taboos and are in an "oral-exploratory" stage of life, where they'll put their mouths on anything. Another says that in a large family, a neglected child may eat dirt to get attention—which assumes the child *is* aware of adult food taboos and violates them on purpose. Other theories hold that a child increases his sense of independence by finding his own "food"; that geophagy is a response to a lack of oral gratification due to a poor mother-child relationship; and even that it represents a child's deliberate attempt to embarrass its mother by making the neighbors think the child isn't being fed properly.

Most societies have regarded eating dirt as weird, but in medieval Europe, eating lettuce was considered weird, too. What we eat and what we don't are often determined more by cultural taboos than by logic. Still, it's probably a good idea to discourage children from eating dirt, which can contain dangerous parasites ("worms") or toxic chemicals.

The CPR Crapshoot

C<small>PR</small> (cardiopulmonary resuscitation) can be performed by lay people with no medical training other than a three-evenings' CPR course, and it does save lives. But not as many lives as you might think.

Artificial respiration, the pulmonary (lung) part of CPR, may date back almost three thousand years. Medical historians cite the biblical story of the prophet Elijah stretching himself out three times on a youth who had just died, and calling on God to bring him back to life, as evidence of the practice around 900 B.C. What we now call CPR, including the stimulation of the heart as well as the lungs, was not invented until 1960.

Even when performed by experienced nurses and doctors, CPR is no cure-all. About half the people who are given CPR in a hospital do not respond to the resuscitation attempt. According to one estimate, only about 20 percent of them survive, recover, and are released, and a small number of those suffer brain damage. (Reported survival rates vary widely, because different researchers have different definitions of cardiac arrest and of long-term survival.)

If everything goes right, a victim of heart attack can have (depending on which estimate you believe) as much as a 40 percent chance of getting out of the hospital alive,

171

even if he's not in the hospital at the time of the attack and CPR is performed by a lay person. If CPR is started within four minutes of cardiac arrest—*and* if it's done correctly *and* if the paramedics can restart the heartbeat on the way to the hospital—then the patient is in the lucky group with the 40 percent chance. That's still a lot better, though, than the chance of survival without CPR.

The Prehistory of Popcorn

THE year is 1000 B.C.; the place, a cave in New Mexico. Some American Indians settle down in front of their fire to prepare a dinner of their most important food . . . popcorn?

Yes, popcorn. These ancient cave dwellers didn't have popping oil, microwave ovens, or artificially flavored buttery seasoning, but they didn't need them. They just poked a stick into an ear of corn and held it over the fire. The kernels popped open but remained attached to the cob.

Corn, together with beans and squash, met all the nutritional needs of many people in the Americas for thousands of years. Corn provides carbohydrates and some protein and fat; beans complement the corn's incomplete protein, and add some vitamins; squash contributes other vitamins and more fat. The combination of the crops (which the southwestern Indians called "the three sisters") is agriculturally efficient and ecologically sound, too. The bean vines grow up corn stalks without hurting the corn, and add nitrogen to the soil. Squash spreads out along the ground, and its leaves keep moisture in the soil and inhibit the growth of destructive weeds.

Scientists recently found some popcorn in a three thousand-year-old garbage heap in a cave. They took the kernels back to their lab, kept them humidified for two days, then dropped them into hot oil. The kernels popped.

You can't pop just any corn, though. There are five basic types of corn, classified according to the proportions of hard and soft starch in their kernels: pop, flint, dent, flour, and sweet corn. (Almost all the starch in popcorn is the hard kind.) These five types are further broken down into over three hundred "races." But all these different kinds of corn are members of the same species, *Zea mays*, which itself is only one of thousands of members of the grass family.

People whose diets consist almost entirely of corn, with few other ingredients, may suffer from pellagra, a disease caused by lack of niacin. But if properly supplemented from time to time, corn can be quite nutritious. The late professor Paul Mangelsdorf, one of the world's leading authorities on corn, said he and his wife would often sit down, like the ancient cave-dwelling Indians before them, to a dinner consisting of nothing but a bowl of popcorn.

Stop Worrying and Love the Bomb

"SURVIVE, Recover, and Win!" was the inspiring motto of the Federal Civil Defense Administration, created in 1950 to tell us what to do when the Russian bombers came. But the agency did such a good job of teaching the public about the horrors of nuclear war that it almost put itself out of business.

Bert the Turtle, the civil defense agency's cute mascot, taught schoolchildren how to "duck and cover" during an air raid. The streets of whole cities were deserted during practice drills. Private industry got into the act, too. For instance, in the 1950s, the National Automobile Dealers' Association produced a short film, *Escape Route*, showing how useful a family car could be in case of atomic war.

But people learned so much about the devastating power of nuclear weapons that many began to question whether civil-defense programs would do much good. If the survivors would envy the dead, many reasoned, what good would it do to survive? By the late 1950s, Congress had deeply cut spending on civil defense.

The idea of cheating the bomb had another heyday before and during the Cuban missile crisis, in 1961 and 1962. The Soviet government had built many shelters for its citizens, and prominent Americans, from President Kennedy to Henry Kissinger (then director of the Defense

Studies Program at Harvard), advocated building shelters here, too—but not at government expense. Uncle Sam supplied information about how to build a family shelter but no money.

Economist John Kenneth Galbraith complained to Kennedy that the shelters were great for suburbanites, who could afford them, but not for city dwellers or poor people. Kennedy's policy, Galbraith said, would save Republicans and sacrifice Democrats.

Private contractors, though, thought the plan was just fine. In 1960, there was only one listing in the Chicago yellow pages under "Air Raid Equipment and Supplies"; by 1962 there were fifty. Banks offered special rates on loans for building fallout shelters. And as debates raged over the morality of shooting neighbors trying to break into your family's shelter, one business advertised decoy air shafts that you could install all around the yard, to confuse anyone trying to find your bunker.

Following the peaceful conclusion of the Cuban crisis, interest in fallout shelters and civil defense never returned to its 1962 level.

Though the U.S. may have gone out of the survival business, other countries are stepping up their efforts to make it safely through Armageddon. The U.S.S.R. has a civil-defense program that deals with natural and man-made disasters as well as wars, but the Chernobyl nuclear accident raised questions about the program's efficiency. Some Western observers think its main purpose is to bolster citizens' devotion and loyalty to the Soviet government.

If you're determined to survive the next world war, Switzerland or the Scandinavian countries might be your best bet. They already have public or government-subsidized shelters for most of their population.

Lunar Legacy

IT cost $40 billion to find out, but now we know what the moon smells like: exploded firecrackers. Apollo 11 astronaut Buzz Aldrin described the odor after noticing that some moon dust had gotten into the lunar module on his boots. That's great to know, but what else did the moon shots tell us about the moon?

Yes, there were spin-offs. Brand-name products like Tang and Teflon and Space Food Sticks were all invented for the Apollo program. There were medical and economic breakthroughs, like computer miniaturization, lightweight artificial limbs, and the telemetry that allows an emergency-room doctor to monitor the vital signs of a patient who's still in an ambulance. Seeing the earth floating in space emphasized the need for peace and environmental protection. And the Apollo project created jobs, jobs, jobs.

These were useful by-products, but Apollo's goal was the moon, remember? After landing there and returning six times, what did Apollo find out specifically *about the moon*?

First, there's no life there, which is a good thing, considering that Aldrin could have inhaled dangerous alien germs while smelling that gunpowder-scented dust. The absence of life on the moon was so clear that NASA didn't even bother to quarantine the astronauts on their return to earth after the third mission (Apollo 14).

Not only is there no life on the moon now, but the evidence suggests there never has been. All the moon rocks brought back by Apollo were igneous (formed from lava). None were sedimentary (made of water-borne mineral deposits)—and water is necessary to life as we know it.

The lifeless moon does, however, contain evidence that life may be quite common in the universe at large. There are simple molecules containing atoms of carbon, oxygen, and nitrogen—atoms that were ejected from the sun and other stars and landed on the moon. In a friendlier environment (on a planet with water, for example), these molecules could have evolved into the complex organic compounds necessary to support life.

Moon rocks returned by Apollo also contained new information about the origin of the universe. Astronomers had already determined that the solar system formed about 4.6 billion years ago, but corroborating evidence on earth was hard to find. Erosion had destroyed all earth rocks older than 3.8 billion years. The *youngest* moon rocks are almost that old, and some lunar material dates back 4.6 billion years, confirming the astronomers' estimate of the solar system's age. (The astronauts dug up some of these oldest rocks by blasting deep into the moon with a standard army grenade launcher.)

An old saying has it that the moon is made of green cheese, and the oldest moon rocks have proved the adage half right. Most lunar material is black, white, or gray, but the color of the oldest samples, which date back to the formation of the solar system, is green. (Actually, "green cheese" doesn't mean cheese that is green in color—although there are some kinds of cheese that are green—but rather, cheese that has not aged enough, cheese that is green in the sense of being unripe.)

Miners as well as cosmologists may benefit from the Apollo astronauts' findings. There are valuable deposits of minerals—including aluminum, titanium, calcium, and magnesium—which could be exploited. There's also plenty of oxygen trapped in moon rocks; if we knew how to extract it, people living on the moon could breathe it and use it to help burn fuel while mining or doing other work.

Some of the astronauts prospected for lunar "gold" without a pickax. Several of them took souvenirs, such as little flags and stamped envelopes to be cancelled on the moon, and although a few donated them to charity after returning to earth, others sold them to collectors. When news of the scheme leaked out, it was explained that the astronauts had planned all along to invest the proceeds in trust funds for their children's education.

Even after the astronauts departed from the moon, devices they left behind continued to send information to earth-bound scientists. Battery- and nuclear-powered seismic monitors gathered data about moonquakes until 1978, when the government cut off the funds necessary to operate them. Selenologists (who study the moon, as geologists study the earth) found that moonquakes happen more often at certain times of the lunar month, possibly because of tidal forces exerted by the earth. A typical moonquake releases an amount of energy equal to the detonation of a firecracker.

From the seismic data, researchers can tell that the moon's outer layers consist of a crust thirty-seven to sixty miles thick and a mantle five hundred miles thick. But the core of the moon remains a mystery—and the makeup of the core is the key to discovering why the moon has no magnetic field today, although it had one billions of years ago. The solution to that puzzle, in turn, could help explain why the earth's magnetic field reverses itself every few thousand centuries. By measuring the reflections of laser beams aimed from earth at precisely positioned mirrors left on the moon by Apollo, scientists can detect tiny wobbles in the moon's motion, from which they may be able to determine the composition of the core. The mirrors don't require power to operate, but they are gradually being covered with dust stirred up by meteor impacts and will not be usable after about a hundred years. Hitting the eighteen-inch-square mirrors requires a good aim: Scientists have to make about a thousand tries per successful reflection.

A NASA commission chaired by astronaut Sally Ride recently urged that the United States resume *manned* lunar exploration. It *is* possible to gather lunar samples with robot probes—the Soviet Union returned two such craft from the moon in the early 1970s with a total of only five ounces of lunar soil—but no machine has the curiosity, the eye for the unexpected, and the ability to interpret facts in context, of the human explorer. The Ride commission gave several suggestions for further lunar investigation. We haven't visited the moon's polar regions, where some scientists think there may be small amounts of water. And there's no known explanation for "lunar transient events"—red mists that have been observed from earth, which may be gases escaping from the moon's interior. These events could provide information about the history of lunar volcanic activity. Ride's report also touted the benefit of additional space-program spin-offs, such as medical research and treatment in low gravity, and astronomical research from a radio telescope on the far side of the moon, where it would be shielded from interference from earth.

Meanwhile, the study of moon rocks continues. Twenty years after the Apollo landings, only half of the 842 pounds of samples have been analyzed. The rest of them are stored in nitrogen gas, to prevent iron in them from rusting. In the years since the Apollo program ended, scientists have developed better methods of determining the age of rocks, so it's fortunate that not all the samples were used up immediately. It may be that the longer scientists wait to do research on the remaining rocks, the more they will ultimately learn.

Buddy, Can You Spare a Trime?

"**D**o you have change for a dollar?" "Sure. Would you like five twenty-cent pieces or thirty threes and a dime?"

Those may sound like the words of a counterfeiter, a practical joker, or just someone not very good at making change, but that transaction could actually have taken place during the 1870s.

The United States has issued coins in several denominations that seem strange to us today, from a half-cent to $50. Some of them met a real need, but others were unnecessary or unpopular and disappeared quickly.

The three-cent piece was issued in 1851, when the postage rate had just been lowered from five to three cents. The trime (its slang name) was supposed to be a convenience for the post office and its customers. But another reason for the coin's existence was the California gold rush. The price of gold dropped sharply as the supply increased, and the price of other precious metals, especially silver, rose. Suddenly, silver coins became more valuable for their metal than for their face value, and many were melted down or hoarded. To meet the resulting coin shortage, the government created the new three-cent coin, which contained less than three cents' worth of silver.

A few years later, a $3 gold coin appeared, to make it easier to pay for a sheet of a hundred stamps. But in the

1870s the price of a stamp fell to 2 cents, and not many more three-cent or $3 coins were minted after that. They weren't completely discontinued until 1889, and they continued to circulate until as recently as the 1920s.

There was less justification for the twenty-cent piece. Politicians gave all sorts of excuses for the creation of this coin in 1875. Perhaps it did make more sense in our decimal system of coinage than the quarter-dollar does. But it was also supposedly going to make it easier to make correct change out in the Wild West, where prices were often expressed in terms of the old Spanish bit (12½ cents). No one ever explained, though, exactly how a twenty-cent piece would be useful in that kind of transaction.

The real reason for the new coin was that senators from silver-producing states had thought it up as a way to increase sales of that metal to the government. The public, however, didn't see much need for the twenty-cent piece, and besides, it was confusing because it looked too much like a quarter, so the mint stopped making it after only four years.

A hundred years later, history repeated itself and the U.S. Mint apparently still hadn't learned its lesson. The Susan B. Anthony $1 coin failed for the same reasons as the twenty-cent piece. The original study proposing the Anthony dollar, prepared by the Research Triangle Institute, had suggested that it be eleven-sided and copper-colored, but the mint made it round and silver, just like the quarter—and just like the doomed twenty-cent piece.

Perhaps the coin with the strangest denomination ever issued in America was the token minted for local use by a copper-mine owner in Connecticut in 1737. People generally treated the token as if it were worth threepence, but the legend on the coin read, "Value me as you please."

A Penny Here, Three Tenths of a Cent There, Pretty Soon It All Adds Up

"COMPUTER Wizard Embezzles Millions—a Penny at a Time!" Sounds like the headline from a supermarket tabloid, and it may be a bit exaggerated. Perhaps these schemes don't net millions, but they *do* succeed on a smaller scale. They're common enough that investigators have a name for them. Because they involve carving off little slices of cash, they're collectively known as the "salami scam."

The classic technique in a salami scam is the "round-down" method, which predates computers. When a bank is crediting interest to its customers' accounts, it usually rounds the amount up or down to the nearest cent. A bank employee might, however, direct the computer to round the amount *down* in all cases and collect an average of half a cent on each account being updated. The sum of these fractional pennies would be deposited into the employee's account or, preferably, an account in a fictitious or friend's name, since bank employees' accounts are audited more closely than other people's.

One embezzler used this trick while figuring salesmen's commissions; he slightly undercalculated each one, then credited the difference to the last salesman on the list, a nonexistent Mr. Zwana. He was caught when the company decided, as a publicity stunt, to give an award

183

to the two employees whose names were first and last alphabetically and went looking for Mr. Zwana.

Other salami scams involve somewhat larger "slices": In one case, an embezzler took about a quarter-dollar from each of three hundred accounts, selecting a different group of accounts each time. Most of the bank depositors, on balancing their checkbooks, ignored the slight discrepancy, assuming they had made an arithmetic mistake. In another scheme, two computer programmers had their fellow employees' tax withholding decreased by 2 cents a month, deposited the pennies in their own withholding account, and were the only smiling people in America come April 15.

Of course, the most successful embezzlers are those who gallop off with the loot and no one's the wiser. The next best thing is for the crime to be discovered but for the criminal to escape. One man, with a little help from his friends, got away with $1 million and has never been caught. He opened accounts at two banks, one in New York and one in California. He then had a printer counterfeit some blank checks that bore the names of these banks but that had the wrong bank routing code numbers on them. He started writing checks to himself on one bank and depositing them in the other. After a few days, the second bank would credit the money to his account. Next, he would write a check on *that* bank and deposit it in the first. Each bank would *credit* the *deposits* to the swindler but never *debited* the *withdrawals* because the checks never cleared. The routing codes printed on the checks were those of a third bank, where the man didn't have an account at all. In each case, when the national automated check-clearing system sent the check to the third bank, an employee there would notice that the name of, say, the New York bank was printed on it and would forward it there. However, once it arrived in New York, the bank's computer would send it back to the third bank because of the incorrect routing code. The fraud wasn't discovered until one of the checks became so tattered, from its circular passage through the mail and machines, that someone looked closely and noticed that the bank name and numbers didn't match. By then the perpetrator was gone.

Please don't try this at home. If you must, however, then at least have a heart, like the New York City bank clerk who embezzled $1.5 million. His methods were crude and he was caught, but at least he'd been careful, initially, to take no more than $10,000 from each account—the maximum amount of federal deposit insurance at the time. When the FDIC later raised its insurance limit to $20,000, he raised his theft limit accordingly but no higher, because he wanted to make sure that no depositor would lose anything when the discrepancies came to light.

The Coffee Cantata

A PLANT was being imported from tropical countries—a plant containing a potent drug which, in its pure state, takes the form of a white powder. Merchants sold paraphernalia connected with its use, and in big cities there sprang up "shops" and "houses" devoted to the substance. Popular music ridiculed parents who objected to their children's experimentation with the stuff.

No, it wasn't America in the 1960s, it was Europe in the early 1700s. The controversial substance wasn't something to smoke or snort, it was a beverage. And the music wasn't Jefferson Airplane's "Go Ask Alice" or Jackson Browne's "Cocaine," it was the "Coffee Cantata" by Johann Sebastian Bach.

Today, more than a billion people drink coffee regularly, but many of them prefer a brew that doesn't contain the white powdery drug, caffeine. Decaffeinated coffee isn't a particularly new invention inspired by recent health concerns. The German coffee firm Hag made the first decaf in 1905.

The outer "waxy" layer of the coffee bean contains a good deal of caffeine, as well as other substances that can irritate the stomach. Europeans drink a lot of *partially* decaffeinated coffee, made by removing this layer.

More complete decaffeination, though, requires removing caffeine from the bean's interior. For decades, this was done with solvents like trichloroethylene, a narcotic and anesthetic that smells like chloroform. The caffeine dissolved in the solvent, then both were removed by steaming the beans. Next, the beans were roasted as usual, while the caffeine was sometimes recovered from the solvent for use in medicines.

In 1964, the U.S. Public Health Service issued a report on air pollution generated by the coffee industry. The main problem was the black, smelly smoke wafting from the roasting beans (whether decaffeinated or regular), but the unfortunate neighbors of these java factories also complained about the stench of the decaffeinating solvents.

Since 1971, the industry has turned increasingly to a safe, odorless gas as its decaffeinating agent—carbon dioxide. This is the "natural effervescence" some coffee advertisements tout.

Unfortunately, even "decaf" contains some caffeine. Still, there's a significant reduction: a typical five-ounce serving of brewed coffee has 85 milligrams (mg) of caffeine; instant, 60 mg; tea, 50 mg; instant tea, 30 mg; cola soft drink, 15 to 30 mg; and decaf, only 3 mg.

How We Know What We Know About Dinosaurs

DINOSAURS are *in*. There are dinosaur picture books, dinosaur stuffed toys, and dinosaur swizzle sticks. An exhibit called "Dinosaurs Alive," featuring moving and growling models of the beasts, recently toured museums around the U.S.

All that has survived of dinosaurs, though, are a few bones and other fossils. How, then, can anyone say with confidence what dinosaurs looked like, how they acted, and what they ate?

Knowledge about dinosaurs is relatively recent, even though people have been finding fossils for hundreds of years. Until the early nineteenth century, fossils were thought to be the ancient remains of animals that still existed in other parts of the world, or perhaps the bones of giant humans.

Then in 1822 an English couple named Dr. and Mrs. Mantell found some huge fossilized teeth among rock-quarry debris that had been thrown out along a road. The Mantells, amateur fossil collectors, knew that their finds did not fit into any existing scientific theory. Their suggestion that the fossils were from an extinct, previously unknown animal they named Iguanadon ("iguana-teeth") at first drew a skeptical response from scientists, but further research gained acceptance for their theory.

By 1841, paleontologists had found fossilized remains of two more species of extinct animals in England. That year, Dr. Richard Owen coined the word *dinosaur*—Greek for "terrible lizard"—to describe the beasts. In 1853, Owen hosted a formal dinner party inside a half-restored Iguanadon skeleton.

Over the past 150 years, scientists have made educated guesses about dinosaurs from many kinds of evidence. Grooves in bones show where tendons were attached, and from this information anatomists can reconstruct the shape of the dinosaurs' muscles. Fossils of skin show that dinosaurs were scaly rather than hairy or feathered.

Fossilized footprints not only tell us the shape of a dinosaur's feet but reveal other information as well. Was a particular species social, or did its individuals go their own ways? Multiple sets of tracks in the same place, made at the same time, suggest that a species traveled in herds. Did they walk on two legs or four? Again, footprints, along with bones showing the length of the front legs, are helpful. (Researchers once found a set of footprints from a dinosaur's front feet but none from the back feet. They decided that the animal must have been floating in water and pushing itself along the bottom with its front paws.)

The shape of a dinosaur's teeth suggests the kind of food it ate. Some species had no teeth at all; their diet may have consisted of insects, eggs, and fruit, either swallowed whole or gummed. Thanks to a stroke of excellent luck, scientists have even found the naturally mummified bodies of a few duck-billed dinosaurs, with their last meal—pine needles, millions of years old—still in their stomachs.

Even when fossil evidence is not available, scientists can make some further guesses about dinosaur physiology. Using their knowledge of evolution, they work backward from the dinosaurs' closest living relatives—birds and crocodiles.

We still don't know whether all dinosaurs were cold-blooded, as today's lizards are; there is evidence on both sides. And we may never know what color dinosaurs were. Some scientists think they may have come in all sorts of bright and vivid hues, like modern-day tropical lizards, instead of the boring grays and greens usually shown in picture books.

Any Resemblance to Persons Living or Dead Is Purely Coincidental— or Not

JOHN Wayne, the Duke, legend of the silver screen, is going to portray you in a movie! To many people, that would be welcome news. But when U.S. Navy commander Robert B. Kelly heard that, he sued—and won.

The movie, filmed in 1945, was *They Were Expendable*, now regarded as one of the finest World War II pictures. The Duke's character was named Rusty Ryan, not Robert B. Kelly. And the standard disclaimer appeared on the screen: "The characters and events portrayed in this motion picture are fictitious. Any resemblance to any person, living or dead, is purely coincidental."

Coincidental or not, Kelly charged that the film depicted him as "headstrong, undisciplined, aggressive, resistant to orders and self-seeking, and in relation to a U.S. Army nurse, as unduly amorous." The judge agreed and, emphasizing that the real Kelly was dutiful, modest, and patriotic, awarded him the verdict. Unfortunately for the naval officer, the judgment against the film's producers amounted to only $3,000 (which, of course, Kelly had to share with his legal counsel).

Admittedly, the case was atypical; though the movie displayed the usual disclaimer, it also stated that it was based on the book by William L. White, in which the characters were identified by their real names. Though unusual in this respect, and despite the meager payoff, Commander Kelly set a precedent that still haunts motion picture producers. No matter how they phrase that "purely coincidental" disclaimer, movie studios and producers may still be liable if there is some noncoincidental connection between a character and a real person. Consequently, studio legal departments do not allow scriptwriters to give a character the same name as a real person living in the city in which the action of a movie takes place.

Rabies

Few diseases are as surrounded by myth and fear as rabies. Most people's understanding of rabies goes something like this: A person is bitten by a mad dog; he then has the choice of "submitting to a long and painful series of injections in the stomach" (as the newspapers love to put it) or else dying in agony after weeks of convulsions, frothing at the mouth, and pathological fear of water; and once the symptoms begin, there's no hope of survival. That scenario turns out to be a mixture of fact, fancy, and misunderstanding.

Animal bites are the most common way humans contract rabies, but there are others. Some Texans were infected while exploring a cave filled with rabid bats in 1956, even though they were not bitten. They had inhaled the virus in the dust of dried bat excrement. A researcher inhaled it while he was grinding up a rabid goat's brain in a blender in 1972. Transplanted tissue from other humans, especially corneas, can also transmit rabies.

Once the rabies virus has infected a person, it stays near the site of infection for a few days before spreading to the brain. That accounts for the moderate success of an ancient Roman remedy, cupping the wound. This involved turning a cup upside down and burning a candle inside it to evacuate some of the air. The cup was then

193

placed over the bite, and as it cooled, a partial vacuum was created, which sucked the virus-rich fluids from the wound.

Fortunately, the human immune system knows how to fight the virus, but unfortunately, the immune response isn't triggered until the virus reaches the brain, by which time it's too late, because by then it's already started to do its damage. Vaccines, however, can make the immune response begin sooner, killing the infection before it spreads. Louis Pasteur created the first rabies vaccine in 1885, and his original viral strain, kept alive in a Paris laboratory, is still used to manufacture rabies vaccine today. In the past, dog-bite victims really did have to undergo the notorious "long and painful series of injections" in the abdomen (not literally in the stomach). They could also have gotten the fourteen to twenty-one injections in the buttocks, but that would have been even worse because it would have made sitting down painful. Modern vaccines require six or fewer shots, which can be given in various parts of the body.

If the virus isn't stopped soon enough, though, the victim will develop the familiar symptoms. Intensive care can prolong life, sometimes for months, but eventually the inflammation of the brain causes the failure of vital organs whose functions cannot be replaced by intensive care.

Death is almost certain after the symptoms appear, but there have been at least three cases of survival—the details of which are still controversial. A six-year-old Ohio child bitten by a bat in 1970 was vaccinated immediately but developed symptoms anyway. He was unconscious for days but recovered fully. Some researchers believe, however, that his symptoms were not caused by rabies but by encephalitis brought on by the rabies vaccine itself. A similar case occurred in Argentina in 1972. A New York medical researcher also survived rabies in 1977; he had been vaccinated before he caught the disease, because of the nature of his work, but even so, he has never recovered fully.

Some parts of the world are completely free of rabies and use strict quarantine laws to stay that way. England has been since 1903; so is the island of Singapore, even though its neighbors have high rates of the disease. Even some non-island countries, like Spain, are rabies-free.

How San Francisco Became the Gay Capital of the United States

In a word-association test, *San Francisco* might elicit the responses *Tony Bennett, earthquake,* or *Golden Gate.* And somewhere near the top of the list would be *homosexual.* How did gays transform San Francisco into a city commonly regarded as the gay capital of America? Surprisingly, it was largely the work of the politicians, bureaucrats, and officers who ran the U.S. military during World War II.

In the late nineteenth century, San Francisco, a city with an anything-goes reputation, had a quiet homosexual community, catered to by special restaurants containing discreet, secluded tables. City leaders began enforcing laws against gays early in the twentieth century, and Prohibition (1920–1933) forced underground gay bars to close.

World War II, and the military's regulations against homosexuals, reversed the gay decline in San Francisco. Soldiers and sailors who were discovered to be gay were immediately discharged from the service—dishonorably, with a big "H" stamped on their papers. Those who had been kicked out of the Pacific theater were transported back to San Francisco and dumped there. Prejudice in their hometowns made it impossible for many of the veterans to return to friends and family, so they stayed put. Since

196

they had already been forced out of the closet, they had nothing further to hide, so many began to live openly as gays.

More or less openly, that is. Even with a growing gay population, San Francisco was not a trouble-free haven for homosexuals in the 1940s. California law made it illegal to serve alcohol to a homosexual or to dress as a member of the opposite sex. So-called drag queens avoided the latter restriction by attaching pieces of paper to their dresses saying "I'm a boy"; the courts accepted the argument that anyone wearing such a notice was technically dressed as a man, not a woman. Many gays arrested under other harassing laws demanded jury trials, endeavoring to overload the court system.

The law notwithstanding, San Francisco police stayed in touch with leaders of the gay community behind the scenes. From time to time, they entered unofficial agreements that helped prevent confrontations. For example, the police agreed to look the other way one night a year: Halloween.

Homosexuality was first raised as a political issue in San Francisco in 1959, by a mayoral candidate demanding stricter enforcement of anti-gay laws. Although he lost the election, city officials increased enforcement against homosexuals to prevent the issue from being used against the incumbents in the future.

But that was the last hurrah for official harassment of gays in San Francisco. In 1961, the first openly gay political candidate in the U.S., Jose Sarria, got seven thousand votes in an unsuccessful run for the city board of supervisors. In the next few years, the votes, money, and other contributions of homosexuals took on more and more importance in San Francisco politics. For example, in 1972, by soliciting signatures from voters in gay bars at one minute past midnight on the first day of the official campaign season, George McGovern managed to have his election petitions turned in to officials before any other candidate's—and thus got his name in the strategic first position on the primary ballot.

Finally, in 1977, Harvey Milk became the city's first openly gay elected official, serving on the board of supervisors until a former board member, Dan White, killed him and Mayor George Moscone a year later.

A Gaggle of Hoons

AMERICANS are wimps. We complain about dirty politics, but aside from a little mudslinging during the election campaign season, our politicians are usually civil and polite to each other, at least on the surface. In Britain and her former colonies, though, they're at each other's throats day in and day out—not just on TV, but in the hallowed halls of Parliament itself.

"Loud-mouthed fatso!" these honourable members of Parliament call each other. "Little weasel!" "Gaggle of hoons!" (*Hoon* is Australian slang for "ruffian.") "You sewer rat!" Even "dickhead!" And these were some of the expressions that were *not* ruled out of order in the various Australian state legislatures where they were hurled. In one case the presiding officer said he was just letting the politicians have what Australians would consider a "fair go" at each other.

Expressions like these are carefully collected by the clerks of all the parliaments in the Commonwealth (the former British Empire) and published each year in *The Table*, a scholarly legal publication that carries articles about the rights, duties, and responsibilities of parliaments and their members—and a list of insults used in the past year. The list tells the date the insult was issued, the name of the country or state, and whether the chair ruled the phrase to be acceptable or not.

Aussie politicians are not unique in their obnoxiousness. Parliaments of other countries show up in *The Table*'s list as well. A member of Canada's Parliament called an official a "sleaze bag." A Zambian representative was ruled out of order when he referred to another politician's taste for "horizontal refreshment." And an honourable in Papua New Guinea's Parliament threatened another, "If you call me 'long-long' [crazy], I will knock your block off."

Sometimes a parliamentarian will call an opponent by an unflattering name or title: "Castro"; "Ivan the Terrible"; "the Minister for Sleaze"; "the Minister of Social Injustice"; "the Libyan Consul-General"; "the voice of the South African Embassy"; or as one Indian politician called Indira Gandhi, "Lady Macbeth." The speakers of most parliaments usually reprimand members who use this tactic.

The official protocol in Parliament is to refer to other politicians not as "Mr. Jones" but as "the Honourable Member for East Norwich" (or whatever town or district he represents). This formula is often turned into an insult: "the Right Honourable Prima Donna Member;" "the Dubious Member for . . ."; and "the little toad from . . ."

Sometimes these political insults don't make much sense to outside observers. A member of Malta's Parliament was reprimanded for saying "you are a paragon of justice," and in an Indian state legislature the term "hero" was ruled to be out of order. Guess you had to be there.

But often the mudslinging is completely straightforward: "Shut your mouth, you old mug!" "Sit down, you drip!" "Pompous twit!" The words "liar" and "bullshit" are especially popular, even though they are usually disallowed. And, from Zambia's Parliament, perhaps the most succinct political statement ever made: "Phew!"

Where There's Smoke, There's Indians (?)

In western movies, Indians are often shown using smoke signals to communicate with each other. Is this just another Hollywood-manufactured cliché, or did the Indians really signal with smoke? Some did, some didn't, and anthropologists have used this fact to develop theories about the origin and advancement of civilization in the Americas.

The Yahgen people, who lived at the southern tip of South America, used smoke signals to summon neighbors whenever a whale was caught or found beached. Families would come from miles around, camp out, and feast on the whale for as long as a month. In what is now the southwestern U.S., smoke signals carried news about the location of a buffalo herd or the approach of enemies. Some of these signals resembled Morse code, with different numbers of long and short puffs carrying different messages.

But smoke signaling was not universal, and anthropologists have been able to determine a lot about ancient American history from the distinction between groups that used it and groups that didn't.

Indian societies that were isolated geographically (at the northern and southern extremes of the Americas) or economically (by virtue of being nonagricultural or nomadic) tended to share a lot of traits—not only smoke signaling

201

but also scalping, games with dice, and certain puberty rites, such as four days of isolation and fasting for girls having their first period, and an initiation ceremony representing death and resurrection for boys.

Apparently, these practices had survived from a single, old (circa 500 B.C.) American Indian culture that was later replaced by a more advanced agricultural way of life. Only the societies at the geographical and economic fringes of the Americas were untouched by this change and kept the old traditions like smoke signaling.

To make smoke signals the way the Indians did, build a fire with green wood, cover it with a damp blanket, and raise the blanket briefly to emit a puff of smoke.

Ancient Injury

THERE was no poison-control hotline to give ancient Athenians a hemlock antidote. There was no Roman emergency room to treat someone unfortunate enough to be stabbed on the Ides of March by his suddenly former friends. These early societies did, however, have a surprisingly wide range of treatments for wounds and injuries—and some of them even worked.

Torn and punctured skin inspired the most, and the most imaginative, remedies. Such injuries require immediate treatment, to stop the bleeding and close up the wound, and then long-term care, to prevent or treat infection.

Most ancient societies knew about the tourniquet—that it would stop bleeding and that it would cause gangrene if left on too long. Very heavy bleeding was always a death sentence, because no one had figured out how to tie off a major artery or vein (and a tourniquet can only stop such bleeding temporarily), until the Romans of the first century A.D. discovered the technique, and even invented hemostatic clamps that hold themselves in place just as modern clamps do.

For less severe cuts, the ancient Greeks would put cold towels near the wound but not directly on it, a procedure that has the approval of modern doctors. They also put *warm* towels around the head, presumably to prevent fainting. They would dress the wound with a woollen puff rubbed with the sap of a fig tree and secure it in place with a wine-soaked bandage.

The sap probably didn't do any good—the Greeks thought it clotted blood when in fact it only clots milk—but the wine was another story entirely. Modern tests show that red wine kills more bacteria than a simple water-alcohol solution of the same strength as the wine. Even de-alcoholized wine will do the trick, but grape juice won't: Fermentation creates *all* of wine's germ-killing agents. Wine's bactericidal action, like its taste, improves with age, up to a point (about ten years). (Port is the most antiseptic wine of all.) But wine's beneficial action is short-lived, so it needs to be reapplied more frequently than a solution of alcohol would.

Frankincense and myrrh were specified in many ancient prescriptions. Frankincense was used mainly as a perfume in ointments—for example, in a Greek salve along with animal fat and the medically active ingredient, zinc oxide. Perfumes were not added for frivolous reasons; they masked the odor of decaying flesh around the wound. Many ancient practitioners wrote that myrrh and other tree resins must be medicinal because resin "heals" wounded trees and because it does not decay. Their reasoning was incorrect; healing a tree is not analogous to healing human flesh, and resin does not impart its lack of decay to skin or anything else it touches. The ancient medical writings suggest that myrrh *did* work (for some other reason), but there have been no modern studies investigating its usefulness.

In Egypt, myrrh was imported from distant lands and was fantastically expensive. So for the patient of average means, the treatment of choice was fresh meat, or honey and animal grease, secured with adhesive tape made of cloth rubbed with tree gum.

Insect mandibles were used in place of stitches to bind

the two sides of a cut together in ancient India. The doctor would take the head off of a large ant and bring its pincers together through the patient's flesh.

In case of a circular wound, the Greeks *enlarged* the puncture to make it noncircular, which sounds counterproductive but actually helped. A round wound heals more slowly than any other shape. To understand why, imagine a group of people standing shoulder to shoulder in a circle, each person representing a cell on the edge of a wound. If you tell them to walk toward the center (that is, as the wound starts to heal), they can't go very far without squeezing some of the people out, and if all are equally strong, *no one* will ever reach the middle. Arrange them in a square, on the other hand, and some will reach the middle, some won't, but they will converge in an X-shaped pattern—which is exactly what the scar from a square wound looks like.

War, of course, stimulated many advances in medical treatment. In ancient India soldiers had no helmets, so the loss of an ear or a nose was frequent on the battlefield. Their doctors learned to graft cheek skin onto the site of a missing ear and to fold down a flap of skin from the forehead to create a reconstructed nose. To make nostrils in the new nose, they inserted reeds into the wound until the skin graft "took."

Arrows with barbed points were especially dangerous weapons because pulling them out worsened the wound. By the first century A.D., however, the Greeks and Romans (we don't know who invented it first) used the "spoon of Diocles" to alleviate the problem. The instrument looked like a shoehorn, or a long thin cone with a slot along one side. Inserted along the shaft of the arrow, it gently spread the wound open, allowing the extraction of the barbed point with as little additional damage as possible.

The Romans also had military hospitals, even at the farthest borders of the empire, in such uncivilized lands as Germany and Scotland. They had a remarkably intelligent design. Although they were large, they were divided into wards holding only four or five men apiece. This not only cut down on nosocomial (hospital-borne) infections but also helped morale by not subjecting the wounded to the cries and moans of hundreds of other patients.

War isn't the only means by which people brutalize each other; there's also sports. The ancient Greeks loved to wrestle, and dislocated each other's joints with great frequency. Popping a bone back into a joint was a simple matter, but when a wrestler suffered the same injury many times, the doctors tried stronger medicine. After replacing the shoulder joint, they would cauterize the athlete's armpit, thinking that the resulting contraction of the skin would hold the bones in place. (They were wrong, but maybe it cut down on the perspiration smells in the locker room.) They also had a complicated device for wrestling a bone back into place, which looked like a rack from the Spanish Inquisition, and apparently caused as many injuries as it cured. For a plain and simple broken bone, rather than a dislocation, the treatment was easy: a splint. The Egyptians knew this at least as long ago as 2500 B.C.

Trepanning the skull, or cutting a hole in it (from the Greek word *trypanon*, meaning "drill"), was done as early as 12,000 B.C. Cultures all over the world, from Europe to South America, have practiced trepanning for a variety of reasons. Some used it to try to relieve the pain of a head fracture, some to let evil spirits out of the brain. In the early twentieth century, an Algerian woman subjected herself to it to fabricate evidence for use in a trumped-up divorce case against an allegedly abusive husband. In primitive times, according to the archaeological evidence, the operation may not have cured anything, but it was almost never fatal. In early nineteenth-century European hospitals, on the other hand, it almost always killed the patient, thanks to nosocomial infections.

One way to avoid infecting a patient with another's

disease is to use disposable needles and other instruments. In the days of the pharaohs, the Egyptians used disposable knives made of sharpened reeds for medical purposes. But it wasn't to avoid infection that the Egyptian doctors threw away their scalpels. They didn't have any permanent, reusable instruments because they had almost no iron to make them from. They hardly knew of the metal, except in very rare cases where the miraculous substance was retrieved from stray meteorites.

Horseshoes Make Horse Sense

Horses got along for millions of years without people nailing curved pieces of metal to their hooves. So who invented the horseshoe, and why?

Ancient Roman writings refer to something called a *hipposandal*, which literally is Latin for "horseshoe." No one is sure exactly what this was, but it is thought to have been something made of leather or cloth to wrap the foot in, not a horseshoe as we know it.

Apparently, the metal shoe for the bottom of the hoof was invented in northern Europe sometime before the year 1000. The muddy soil and sod of those cold, rainy climates mired down horses' hooves and caused them to rot. Furthermore, the winter ice kept them from getting a good footing in freezing weather.

In addition to helping horses work for people, horseshoes have taken on symbolic meanings. President George Bush pitched horseshoes to try to convince us that he was just plain folks. And for centuries the horseshoe has been a symbol of good luck. How it got that connotation isn't clear, but veterinarian and anthropologist Elizabeth Atwood Lawrence of Tufts University has some ideas: The horseshoe's shape resembles other, older, traditional good-luck charms, such as the arch, horns, and crescent moon; the shoe is powerful because it is in direct contact with a live, growing thing (the hoof), but also helps to protect and regulate its growth; the nailing of the shoe to the hoof calls forth an association with Christ. Professor Lawrence admitted that these theories were merely her own suggestions, without much evidence to support them. Many reviewers of her book on the subject found them a bit farfetched.

If there are horseshoes, are there also horse socks? As a matter of fact, there are. Urban police horses often wear a pad between hoof and shoe. This practice gives the officer an extra couple of inches' height advantage over a crowd.

Caste for Converts

IF you converted to the Hindu religion, what caste would you belong to? And in the modern, secular republic of India, what difference would it make anyway?

The Hindu faith doesn't actively seek converts. This, according to one Indian historian, is largely because it is an ethnically based religion, but also because Hindus are more interested in "the increase in righteousness . . . raising man from his level of experience to a higher level of experience," than acceptance of a formal creed.

Still, it *is* possible to convert to Hinduism. And even though India's constitution guarantees religious freedom, there are still legal consequences to religious conversion, especially conversion *from* Hinduism to other faiths. When the British ruled India, their law prohibited the courts from enforcing these sanctions, but independent India passed a Hindu Marriage Act in 1955 reinstating them. Under this law, a convert to the Hindu, Buddhist, Jaina, or Sikh religion is a Hindu for legal purposes. The legal distinction between Hindu and non-Hindu saved at least one defendant from a prison sentence. In 1944, a Mr. Munuswami, born a Hindu, converted to Christianity in order to marry a Christian woman he had been having an affair with. Five years later, though, he reconverted to Hinduism and (without divorcing his first wife) married a Hindu. A prosecutor charged him with bigamy, which at the time was legal for Hindus but illegal for Christians. The judge ruled that Munuswami was a Hindu and therefore innocent.

Indian courts recognize a variety of evidence that a person is a Hindu: taking part in a formal conversion ceremony, using a Hindu name, celebrating Hindu festivals, marrying in accordance with Hindu rituals. None of these actions is required, however. In the bigamy case mentioned above, Judge Panchapakesa Ayyar of the Madras high court ruled that "the religious persuasion of a man nowadays depends on his 'subjective preference' for any religion," and that "even a few hours will be enough if the intention to leave one religion and embrace another can be inferred beyond all reasonable doubt."

Conversion is legally recognized, then, but what about the convert's caste? Caste membership is still vitally important in the political, economic, and social spheres. Many Indians will not marry someone outside their own caste. Political parties and associations are often caste-based. And caste still influences the occupation a person may go into, although much less than in the past.

There are an estimated three thousand or more castes and subcastes in India, but five main divisions of society, which traditionally were responsible for particular functions. In descending order of status, they are the Brahmins (priests and intellectuals), Kshatriyas (rulers and military leaders), Vaisyas (farmers and merchants), Sudras (laborers), and the untouchables. This least privileged group, also called outcastes (because they belong to no caste) or Harijans ("children of God," a term coined by Mahatma Gandhi), had to do the most unpleasant jobs, such as waste disposal. They also performed any task that required killing animals or using their carcasses, such as fishing and tanning hides. Members of other castes still commit thousands of caste-related acts of violence against Harijans every year.

The caste system began as simple ethnic discrimination, with the lighter-skinned, northern, immigrant Aryans on top, and the darker-skinned, southern, indigenous Dravidians on the bottom. Later, an ideology grew up around it, defending it as an economic system for the division of labor and the prevention of unemployment, with each caste responsible for particular occupations. It was also touted as a religious system emphasizing the interdependence of all people. But in practice, castes often put their own interests before those of society as a whole, and the system stifled individual advancement and social mobility.

A convert to Hinduism generally becomes a Sudra, a member of the lowest division of castes (excepting the outcastes). But that's just the general rule. Each caste has its own ruling council and can admit anyone it pleases. If you can talk the Brahmins into accepting you, you can start at the top, not near the bottom, of Indian society. Even if a convert does not join any caste at all, he or she can still be recognized as a Hindu under the law.

Vice versa, it's not necessary to adhere to the Hindu religion to be a member of a caste, either. Many castes, reflecting their origin as occupational groups, consist of Hindus *and others* who have kinship ties or practice the same vocation. Even the pews in some Christian churches in India are segregated by caste.

The Mystery of the Freemasons' G

Scottish poet Robert Burns (1759–1796) wrote a poem about it, and today it is on display in many good-size towns in the English-speaking world.What is it? Burns describes it as ". . . that hieroglyphic bright,/Which none but craftsmen ever saw." In other words, it's the letter G inside a compass and a square—the symbol of the Freemasons.

When Burns said "craftsmen," he meant those initiated into the craft of Masonry; and when he said that none but they ever saw it, he obviously didn't mean it literally—the symbol hangs outside as well as inside Masonic temples—but rather, that only Masons see it with full understanding of what it signifies.

Does this mean that non-Masons are not supposed to know what the letter G stands for? Many people think so. Some say the letter stands for God, others say it stands for something else, but it's generally thought that the identity of the G-word is one of those secrets that a Mason must (as one Masonic saying goes) "ever conceal, never reveal."

In fact, ever since the symbol was introduced, around 1760, the Masons have never concealed the fact that their G stands for two words at once: *God* and *geometry*—the latter being the science necessary to brickmasons and other builders, and the former being the greatest "builder" of them all.

But even though the Masons let us outsiders know what their G stands for, there is apparently some additional mumbo-jumbo associated with the G-compass-square symbol that is available only to the society's members. So Burns was right when he said that "none but craftsmen . . . ever saw" the "hieroglyphic" with full understanding of its meaning.

A Busy Beaver Is Hard to Find

Some of the best engineers and builders in the world are beavers. Working together, they can build dams over two thousand feet long out of poles, river debris, or even (in the Dakota badlands, were there are no trees) chunks of coal. The dams can create ponds of up to a hundred acres or canals that flow in whatever direction the beavers wish. But why do they go to all that trouble?

Beaver dams serve two purposes: protection and transportation. The fat little rodent with its stubby legs can't travel very fast on land but is agile in water. The more water a beaver has available, the safer it is from its enemies. And whenever a beaver colony needs to bring food (bark and twigs) from far away, floating it downstream is much easier than dragging or carrying it on land.

A dam usually begins with poles placed in a stream, parallel to the water's flow, with the downstream ends anchored in the mud. Sometimes that's all there is to it; debris floating downstream collects among the poles, and the dam finishes itself. Otherwise the beavers fill it in with mud and whatever else they can find. Often they use an old flooded-out dam as a foundation. Some dams are rebuilt and enlarged over generations.

The dam is not the same as the beaver house or lodge, although they're made of the same materials. A typical beaver house is a dome, surrounded by water, rising as much as six feet above the surface. The only entrance is under water, so the beaver can live in the air pocket under the dome, safe from predators.

Beavers are resourceful, but the cliché notwithstanding, they aren't constantly "busy"—far from it. They spend most of their time playing, according to Al Milotte, who photographed a Disney nature film about beavers in Alaska. Milotte wanted to shoot some footage of a beaver felling a tree with its teeth, but it was several weeks before one of the creatures got busy and obliged him.

I Dismember Mummy

*A*utopsy. The Greek root of that word can mean "see for yourself." But it can also mean "look at yourself." The ambiguity of the word's meaning parallels the many uses and functions of the actual procedure. Originally a way to learn basic facts about the human body, the autopsy today can help police investigators, historians of ancient civilizations, and pollution researchers.

A modern autopsy room looks much like a hospital operating room. Doctors doing an autopsy first examine the outside of the body carefully. Then they make a horizontal incision across the chest and, from there, a vertical incision down the front of the body to the crotch. They remove the ribs and expose the thoracic (heart and lungs) cavity and the abdomen, so that all the organs from the windpipe to the bowels are visible. They cull each organ in turn, weigh it, examine it, and perhaps keep parts of some of them for further research. In what some autopsy observers describe as the most awesome part of the procedure, they cut off the top of the skull, exposing the brain. They remove and inspect it, and formerly kept the pituitary gland so that its human growth hormone (somatotropin) could be used to help patients with growth disorders. (The invention of artificial growth hormone in the 1980s has made this unnecessary.) When the autopsy is finished, they put back everything they don't need to keep, sew up the incisions, and perhaps mark the location of the large arteries for the convenience of the embalmer.

In the 1950s, half of all people who died in hospitals were autopsied, but today, it's only one out of eight. An autopsy costs about $1,000 to perform, and government policies intended to lower hospital costs have reduced the number of autopsies a hospital can afford.

Some pathologists object to these cutbacks because they say autopsies are still very useful. Autopsies can help control epidemics by detecting contagious diseases; improve the quality of health care by uncovering mistakes or shortcomings in a hospital's treatment of a patient; and reassure family members as to the actual cause of a relative's death.

An autopsy is not the blood-spattering, revolting butchery some people assume it to be. In 1861, Dr. Robert Lyons wrote that if done carefully, an autopsy could be performed "in your best dress suit, with only the cuffs of your coat and shirt-sleeves turned up."

Because many ancient societies had taboos against violating dead bodies, they generally did not perform autopsies. The ancient Egyptians *did* invade the body to embalm and mummify it. They carefully removed some of the organs, wrapped them, and put them back into the cadaver, and pulled the brains out through the nostrils with a metal hook. But they didn't gather any medical data along the way. The ancient Hebrews, however, may have learned a good deal about human anatomy by extrapolating the knowledge they got from examining animal carcasses for defects that would make the meat non-kosher (such as perforations of the heart or lungs).

A priest in Haiti performed an autopsy of sorts in 1533, when he dissected the bodies of two dead Siamese-twin children to determine whether they had contained one or two souls. He found two hearts, two livers, four lungs, and so on, and concluded that there had therefore been two souls. The priest's verdict may be taken with a grain of salt, however, because he had a financial interest in the outcome. The whole incident began when the infants' father refused to pay the fee for two baptisms, claiming that the pair of babies was only one child with a single soul.

The scientific use of autopsies began in the early eighteenth century at the University of Padua in Italy. For hundreds of years, European doctors had followed the teachings of the ancient writer Galen (A.D. 130–200), whose medical theory was based on the balancing of four bodily humors (blood, black bile, yellow bile or choler, and phlegm). However, a professor at Padua's medical school, Giovanni Battista Morgagni, argued that there was a connection between disease and visible abnormalities in the body. This is obvious today but was a revolutionary theory at the time. Morgagni and his colleagues and successors used autopsies as a means to gather data for his system of medicine. Today, the preserved skulls of Morgagni and other dead professors gaze down at Padua's medical students in the room where they take their final exams.

The autopsy became such a popular technique in medical education that a minor industry of grave robbers (nicknamed resurrectionists), selling their wares to medical schools, flourished in eighteenth-century Britain. Such activities were illegal in England but not in Scotland: It was against the law there to steal the corpse's clothes, which were the property of the heirs, but not to steal the corpse itself.

In the nineteenth century, Dr. Karl Rokitansky of the Vienna General Hospital was the undisputed king of the autopsy. He examined thirty thousand corpses, giving each one a thorough going-over and taking detailed notes.

It was through such investigations that medical science learned facts we take for granted today. In 1886, for example, doctors using autopsies discovered that severe inflammation of the bowels, often fatal, was caused by the rupture of the appendix. On discovering this, doctors began removing the appendix when the first symptoms of the disease occurred, and the death rate from appendicitis quickly fell.

Back then, new discoveries from autopsies came at a fast and furious rate. By now, we've learned about all we can from autopsies about the cause of disease, although an autopsy does still occasionally reveal new information about AIDS and other illnesses. For the most part, the autopsy has moved on from its original purpose to become a useful tool in many other areas of study.

Autopsies don't necessarily have to occur immediately after death. Thousands of Egyptian mummies were exhumed and autopsied when the first Aswan dam was being built, around 1900, but many of them were only hastily examined. In 1973, though, a mummy nicknamed Pum II (for Pennsylvania University Museum) got the benefit of an autopsy with all the modern conveniences, including videotaping of the whole procedure, at Wayne State University in Detroit. The doctors first X-rayed Pum, a five-foot four-inch man in his late thirties who died around 170 B.C., and then unwrapped him. His brain, kidneys, bladder, and testicles had been removed during embalming, but his eyes were still in their sockets. His spleen, intestines, and lungs had been wrapped and put back into the body cavity, and his penis was propped upright with a piece of wood. Pum's skin, light brown at first, darkened quickly on exposure to the air. He had apparently suffered from roundworms—the doctors found a worm egg in the intestines.

Examinations of other mummies revealed that the earliest Egyptians didn't get cavities in their teeth but later ones did. Apparently, as the nation grew richer, more people were able to afford the luxury of sweets, and tooth decay flourished.

The native people of Alaska didn't mummify their dead, but the climate sometimes did. Several frozen bodies dating from about the year 1500 have been autopsied. Modern Eskimos often suffer from osteoporosis (brittle bones), and one theory holds that a switch from their traditional foods to a more Western-style diet has introduced the condition. But the five-hundred-year-old frozen bodies had osteoporosis, too, casting doubt on that theory.

Very little cancer has been found in any autopsied bodies from long ago, even though cancerous tumors are better preserved by mummification than many other kinds of tissue. Maybe it's because people in times past were exposed to fewer cancer-causing substances than we are today, or maybe it's just because people died of other diseases—that we can cure today—before they had a chance to develop cancer. Autopsies of Chileans who lived around 800 B.C. have exonerated wood fires from responsibility for the presence of dioxins and dibenzofurans (cancer-causing substances) in the human body. Archaeological evidence shows that these Chileans must have breathed a good deal of wood smoke, but their bodies contained much less dioxin than ours do today. Paleopathologists (doctors who autopsy ancient bodies) suggest that wastes from modern industry, not smoke from wood stoves, are responsible for dioxin pollution.

Public-health researchers use autopsy results to learn about modern health risks associated with unsafe working conditions. Paleopathology, though, may have discovered the world's first occupational disease: Many ancient Egyptians had skull ulcers from carrying water jugs on their heads.

Thanks—And an Invitation

WE'VE only just begun. For an encore, we'd like to address the wonders, plunders, and blunders *you* would especially like to read about. If you have any questions or topics you'd like to see included in our next book, please send them to:

Bruce Tindall and Mark Watson
P.O. Box 447
Morrisville, North Carolina 27560

If you're the first person to send in a suggestion we use, we'll send you a free copy of the book in which we answer it, and we'll thank you in print.

Many people helped us research this book, and we'd like to thank them now. Everyone's help was valuable, but there are three people who went far beyond the call of duty and deserve extra-special recognition:

• The Honourable H. G. Smith, Clerk of the Legislative Assembly of the Northern Territory, Darwin, Australia.
• Dr. William H. Gurley, orthodontist and race-car driver, Raleigh, North Carolina.
• The Honourable A. M. Bhattachargee, Justice of the High Court, Calcutta, India.

We are also grateful to the people in the publishing industry who shepherded this book from authors to readers: our agent, Jim Trupin, and everyone at William Morrow and Co., especially Randy Ladenheim-Gil, senior editor.

Further thanks to these people, who helped us bring you the answers we sometimes thought we might never find:

Gernot M. R. Winkler, U.S. Naval Observatory; Eva Wagner, Irvin Industries; Jane Vogel, Perkins Library, Duke University; John A. Toebes, VIII, SAS Institute Inc.; E. Clark Rumfelt, attorney, Jackson, Mississippi; Dee Stuckey and Suzanne Porter, Health Sciences Library Rare Book Collection, University of North Carolina at Chapel Hill; Dr. Everett Pannkuk, orthodontist, Raleigh, North Carolina; Sue McGrath, R.N., formerly of Duke University Medical Center; Prof. Robert Nelson, School of Dentistry, University of North Carolina at Chapel Hill; David Nathanson, National Park Service; Clyde R. Moore, International Boundary Commission (United States–Canada); Frederick C. Mish, Merriam-Webster, Inc.; Prof. Paul Mangelsdorf (deceased), Harvard University; George Kyle, National Park Service; Nick Komons, Federal Aviation Administration; Laura C. Joehl, *Equus* magazine; Edgar Ingram, North Carolina Department of Agriculture; Bruce Horne, Family Egg Market; Prof. I. B. "Bill" Holley, Duke University; Willis G. Haugen, attorney, Newnan, Georgia; Ardie Ferrill, California Department of Food and Agriculture; John P. Felt, U.S. Department of State; Douglass Farnsley, attorney, Louisville, Kentucky; The Honorable Steven E. Ebat, Assistant Attorney General, Wisconsin; Judy du Cellier, U.S. Department of Agriculture Germplasm Services Laboratory; William K. Davis, U.S. Bureau of Alcohol, Tobacco, and Firearms; Helen Crumpler, News Bureau, University of North Carolina at Chapel Hill; David E. Crawley, Jr., attorney, Kosciusco, Mississippi; Harry Y. Canter, National Cancer Institute; Prof. Alan Beck, Purdue University; His Excellency Niels E. Andersen, Danish Consul, Washington; and these institutions: Johns Hopkins University Hospital News Bureau; Marshall Space Flight Center; New York Stock Exchange Public Information Office; and the eighteen different general and specialized libraries we consulted at the Research Triangle universities.

We wish to acknowledge our obligation to friends for their criticism, and particularly to Bruce's wife, Sue McGrath, for improvement of phrase and construction.

For helpful comments and review, and most importantly for their encouragement along the way, we thank Bruce's sister, Blair Alston Mercer Tindall, along with the rest of the orchestra of the Broadway musical *Aspects of Love*; his parents, George and Blossom, and sisters-in-law, Kim Millin and Pat Hale; Mark's parents, Gene and Mary; his sister, Mary, and brother, Steve; New York percussionist and idea-monger Maya Gunji; Poughkeepsie (and Galapagos Islands) attorney Vincent Teahan; and our many friends at SAS Institute, especially Susan O'Connor.

B.M.T.
M.E.W

Index